praise for the FREAK FACTOR

David Rendall reclaims the term "freak" for what it is—a powerful, game-changing, competitive advantage in life and business. This book will change the way you think about being different and show you how it's the secret to turning around your career and the economy.

—Pam Slim, author of *Escape from Cubicle Nation*

The Freak Factor is an important idea, and David Rendall's is a voice to be reckoned with. We should all look to our workplaces and lives to see how we can accommodate rather than eliminate the freaks and the freaky ideas!

—Nick Morgan, author of *Trust Me: Four Steps to Authenticity and Charisma*

Everything you've read about weakness is wrong … until now. This book will help you stop trying to be well-rounded and start excelling at what you always knew you were best at. Raise your freak flag and wave it with pride!

—Chris Guillebeau, author of *The Art of Non-Conformity*

the
FREAK
FACTOR

the
FREAK
FACTOR

d!scovering un!queness
by flaunt!ng weakness

We do not believe in ourselves until someone reveals that deep inside us something is valuable,

worth listening to, worthy of our trust, sacred to our touch.

—e.e. cummings

dav!d j. rendall

Published by Advantage, Charleston, South Carolina.
Member of Advantage Media Group.

ADVANTAGE is a registered trademark and the Advantage colophon is a trademark of Advantage Media Group, Inc.

Printed in the United States of America.

ISBN: 978-1-59932-669-6
LCCN: 2015950589

Front cover photo and flap photo by Dia Worling.
Back cover photo by Erik Smith, HSP Imaging.
Book design by George Stevens.

This publication is designed to provide accurate and authoritative information in regard to the subject matter covered. It is sold with the understanding that the publisher is not engaged in rendering legal, accounting, or other professional services. If legal advice or other expert assistance is required, the services of a competent professional person should be sought.

Advantage Media Group is proud to be a part of the Tree Neutral® program. Tree Neutral offsets the number of trees consumed in the production and printing of this book by taking proactive steps such as planting trees in direct proportion to the number of trees used to print books. To learn more about Tree Neutral, please visit www.treeneutral.com. To learn more about Advantage's commitment to being a responsible steward of the environment, please visit www.advantagefamily.com/green

Advantage Media Group is a publisher of business, self-improvement, and professional development books and online learning. We help entrepreneurs, business leaders, and professionals share their Stories, Passion, and Knowledge to help others Learn & Grow. Do you have a manuscript or book idea that you would like us to consider for publishing? Please visit advantagefamily.com or call 1.866.775.1696.

To Stephanie, Anna, Emma, and Sophia

ACKNOWLEDGMENTS

I want to start by thanking Elliott Anderson. He was the first person who recognized the positive aspects of my seemingly negative characteristics. He is also the first person who called me a freak.

Tom Morris was very influential in the development of this book. He shared countless quotes and articles that supported my idea that weaknesses can be strengths. My friend Stosh Walsh was also extremely helpful because of his deep understanding of the strengths revolution and positive psychology. My weekly conversations with Joel Rodell have been energizing, and my discussions with Allan Bacon have kept me motivated and focused. Joseph Sherman's consistent correspondence was also invaluable.

Kate Mytty, Jon Mueller, and Todd Sattersten at 800-CEO-Read were some of the first people outside of my circle to embrace the freak factor. They supported the creation of the first manifesto and introduced me to many other like-minded people. Pam Slim and Dan Pink have each contributed to this project in a variety of ways. The books of Chris Guillebeau, Parker Palmer, Seth Godin, Ken Robinson, and Marcus Buckingham profoundly affected my understanding of life and career success.

I appreciate the many people whom have commented on my blog and interacted with me on Twitter and Facebook. Their support for the freak factor message has been tremendously encouraging. Some of them are profiled in the book, but I want to list them here as well: Matt Langdon, John Wambold, Craig Houston, Bart Gragg, Clemens Rettich, Jeff Brainard, Leah Shapiro, Zane Safrit, Curt Liesveld, Jurgen van Pletsen, Margie Goodchild, Andrew Galasetti, Lance Haun, Chris Ferdinandi, Kate Schreimer, Nellie Felipe, Joe Heuer, Kelly Wall, Jennifer Schuchmann, Sara Dunnigan, Erika Lyremark, Mary Sailors, Amber Osborne, Scott Priestley, Matthew Peters, Roxy Allen, Jean-Philippe Touzeau, and Elad Sherf.

Many people whom I don't know well have shaped the content of this book by participating in my seminars and classes and responding to my surveys and polls. I have also built some great relationships through my work as a speaker and trainer. Deb Pattison, Susan Barbee, Nick and Nikki Morgan, Don Wells, and Esmond Harmsworth have all been instrumental in the success of my business.

My friends and family have also been very supportive, especially Earl Worley, Bryce Verhaeghe, Mike Ammons, and my mother-in-law, Susan Ford. Finally, this book would not have been possible or meaningful without the love, confidence, and assistance of Stephanie, Anna, Emma, and Sophia.

OUTLINE

FOREWORD

This is a great book about the incredible, outrageous, freakishly wonderful possibility of being exactly who you are—not what someone else may want you to be—and using your amazing distinctiveness to find your own personal form of truly satisfying success.

We all have dreams. But people around us often tell us to "be more realistic." When they give us this advice, what they usually mean is that we should buy into the same assumptions and prejudices about the world that they and people they know have absorbed, without sufficient reason. They want us to accept life as they believe it to be and do more to "fit in." They think that those of us who dream and hope and believe in the rich abundance of new possibilities are deluded and disconnected from reality. But it just may be that an atrophy of their own sensibilities has limited their thinking to a shrunken view of reality. Their world may be the emotional size of a postage stamp, but yours need not be limited at all.

Being properly realistic in our lives and careers doesn't have to mean conforming to the world's most easily available and ready-made patterns; rather, it can mean trusting our own innate instincts to guide us to what's right for us as the individuals we are. The greatest advice echoing down through the centuries from the ancient world may be the commandment "Know thyself!" This means knowing not only your passions, joys, and obvious strengths but knowing your weaknesses as well and considering the possibility that some of those "weaknesses" may really be the keys to hidden strengths that can unlock the doors of astonishing new adventures.

If you go out to a golf course and tee off with a basketball, you can be sure that you won't be getting a hole-in-one. In fact, you'll never sink a single putt. It's not that there is anything inherently wrong with the basketball; it just deserves a different context where its features are perfect. To see what I mean, try dribbling a golf ball down a basketball court on a fast break and taking a three-point shot right before the buzzer. You could be using the best golf ball available, but this is clearly the wrong setting for its qualities.

In this book, David Rendall will show you how to be yourself, in all your glorious you-ness, and how to find the right context or setting that fits you like a glove, even if you have to create that context for yourself—which is often a pretty good idea anyway.

Here's the very good news: you are a freak of nature. There is no one else in the world who can exactly replicate your unique combination of genetics, background, and personal experience. You are one of a kind. There has never been and never will be another you. This book will help you to make the most of this astonishing fact in your life and work.

The ideas in this book stand in a rich, long tradition, which started perhaps with Socrates, was reinvented later by Seneca, got refocused along the way by Søren Kierkegaard, and then hit the shores of America in the work of Ralph Waldo Emerson. Its messages are consistent: do not cave in to false pressures. Break the artificial chains of the past. Don't conform to the crowd.

The ultimate value of aping others can be clearly discerned by a careful consideration of the verb itself. Liberate yourself from average expectations and arbitrary limitations. Be true to yourself. Embrace the glorious freak within. And then, bring the world the greatest gift you can give the rest of us—you, in your own elegantly idiosyncratic form of excellence.

This marvelous, fun, and engaging little book will show you how.

Tom Morris,
philosopher and author of such books as *True Success* and *If Aristotle Ran General Motors*

PART ONE:

THINK

DIFFERENTLY

0. AWAKENING

• •

You may have noticed that this is page 74. Don't worry. It's not a mistake.

The pages are numbered this way on purpose. I'm an achiever. I like to get things done. I like to finish stuff.

But sometimes when you start a book, it can feel like you'll never finish. You read for a while and you're only on page 45 of 223. It seems like you're not getting anywhere.

That's why this book starts on page 74. When you start reading, you'll immediately feel like you've made a lot of progress and you'll impress anyone who asks you what page you're on.

"I'm already on page 74."

"Really? Already. Wow. You're a fast reader."

What Is Your Biggest Weakness?

While researching ideas for this book, I did a Google search for "strengths and weaknesses." The majority of the results were instructions on how to properly answer the interview question, "What is one of your weaknesses?" It is worth noting that this is one of the most common questions asked by interviewers.

The advice that I found falls into three categories. First, tell them about a weakness that you have already improved upon and explain your plan for continued improvement. For example, you could explain that you struggle with new technology but have started playing a lot of online video games to help you get more comfortable with computers and the Internet.

Second, discuss a weakness that is unrelated to the job. For example, in an interview for a job as a construction worker, you could admit to having poor computer skills.

Third, focus on a weakness that has an upside for the company. For example, you could confess that you work too hard and would be so committed to the company that you wouldn't ever take time to relax.

All this advice seems to assume that you have something to hide from the interviewer and are trying to keep him or her from discovering who you really are. If you are successful, then you'll be rewarded with a job and a boss who assumes you either don't have any relevant weaknesses or are willing and able to fix any of your weaknesses.

Once you have the job, most managers keep asking the question about your biggest weakness in the annual performance evaluation. This is because many companies require that evaluations focus on performance issues, developmental challenges, or areas for improvement. All of these are terms to describe weaknesses.

Organizations often require their managers to find and document weaknesses and to create plans for fixing them as part of the evaluation process. In fact, this is usually seen as the primary purpose of the evaluation. The positive aspects of the employee's performance are quickly reviewed or acknowledged, and then the majority of the time is spent on repairing flaws.

We know that employees dread their performance reviews but that evaluations are also one of the tasks that supervisors like the least. This is probably because performance reviews are so negative, and doing them the way I've just described doesn't actually improve performance. As a result, supervisors usually complete the review process as a formality required by the human resources department.

To make matters worse, many companies now use 360-degree feedback tools that allow everyone to participate in the evaluation process. Instead of only being put down by your boss, you can now get criticism from your boss, your peers, and your subordinates.

WE ARE ALL APT TO BELIEVE WHAT THE WORLD BELIEVES ABOUT US.

—George Eliot

De-Forming Beliefs

There are four beliefs that contribute to our feelings of stress and frustration in our relationships and careers. First, we believe that to be successful, we need to be normal: to fit in and not stand out. This means that we should follow the rules and do what we're told. Second, we think that we should be flexible, balanced, and well-rounded by fixing our weaknesses and improving our flaws. Third, we're convinced that we could fit in if we just tried hard enough. Finally, we believe that we could fix our weaknesses if we just had enough self-discipline and perseverance.

All these beliefs seem empowering, but they are actually debilitating. They tell us that we have the potential to succeed, but they mislead us as to where that potential lies and how we should apply it. They set us up for failure and lead to confusion and disappointment when we don't achieve our goals. This creates a downward spiral, as we keep relying on the same incorrect beliefs and ineffective actions to correct the problems that those beliefs and actions created in the first place.

Negative Psychology

The roots of all these myths and counterproductive behaviors can be found in psychology. For more than one hundred years, psychologists have been identifying, diagnosing, and treating our mental disorders. Based on the medical model of identifying and repairing illness, psychology has a negative focus. Counselors and psychiatrists are trained to find and fix our weaknesses. They don't study mental health; they study mental illness. They don't study happiness; they study depression. They don't diagnose satisfaction and fulfillment; they diagnose disappointment and pain.

This approach to psychology might not be so bad if it were actually working. The past one hundred years of medicine has virtually eliminated some diseases (such as polio), discovered preventive measures and treatments for many other previously deadly conditions, and produced a tremendous increase in life span and quality of life. In other words, medical science has helped us to become healthier.

Psychology can't claim the same successes. No cures for mental illnesses have been discovered in the history of psychology. There has been no decrease in mental illness and no rise in mental health. In fact, it is quite the opposite. If anything, psychology has produced a dramatic increase in the number of people who would identify themselves as depressed, anxious, or obsessive.

The default assumption is that there is probably something wrong with all of us and that it probably wouldn't hurt to talk to a counselor about it. But I think it probably does hurt. Talking to a counselor just reinforces our belief that we are different and that we should work harder to be more normal. It also encourages us to focus time, energy, and effort on discovering and deleting our liabilities.

In general, I think psychologists overdiagnose and overmedicate mental illness. In other words, they convince us that something is wrong when there's nothing wrong, and then they give us a pill to fix our supposed sickness. The only guarantee is that the side effects of the medication will probably be worse than our original symptoms. The overall effect is that we have become a society that is dominated by the negative psychological paradigm. We no longer think to challenge the assumptions of this view, even though it has failed to help us live better lives.

Self-Destruction Books

The self-improvement book and seminar industry has a track record similar to that of psychology. The whole industry is built on telling you what is wrong with you, getting you to feel guilty about your shortcomings, and then selling you a solution to your problems. Again, self-improvement seems like a very empowering thing to do. But given the dramatic increase in the number and availability of self-help resources, why don't we see an equal increase in people's performance?

Why do most of the self-help books in this century offer the same advice as those written in the last century? Why do self-help books in this century try to fix the same problems that we had in the last century? Why haven't we made any progress?

We haven't made any progress because self-improvement is based on the same foundation as psychology. Are you disorganized? Read a book on how to be more organized. Are you too shy? Go to a seminar on how to be more outgoing. Are you a pushover? Take a class on how to be more assertive. What could be simpler? But if it is so simple, then why are so many of us still struggling?

The fact is that millions of messy people read books on how to be more organized and try to apply what they've learned, but they just can't. Millions of shy people attend seminars on how to be more outgoing and try to implement what they've been taught, but they just can't. Millions of nonconfrontational people take classes on how to be assertive and try to stand up to others, but they just can't. What's their problem? Why can't they change? Why isn't self-help helping? Is it possible that self-improvement is actually self-destructive?

One Question

As a college professor, I taught classes on personal effectiveness, strategic planning, and managing change. I tried to help people improve their personal lives and their organizations. Over the years, I asked a lot of students to explain why they failed to make important changes in their lives or failed to achieve their goals. One of the common answers was a lack of self-control. Person after person described a sincere desire to improve but an inability to carry it out.

The goal of the class was to help students overcome the barriers to successful planning and meaningful change.. Most strategic planning in an organization starts with a SWOT analysis, which is an exploration of the organization's strengths, weaknesses, opportunities, and threats. Similarly, most guides to self-improvement stress the importance of self-awareness. We need an honest and relatively complete understanding of ourselves in order to grow and succeed.

However, I've found little guidance from the self-improvement industry to help people understand what to change and what to plan. What should people do with their self-awareness? What kinds of things should we try to change? What if there are some things that we can't or shouldn't change? Specifically, when confronted with our strengths and weaknesses, how should we respond?

I believe strongly in our ability to learn and grow. However, I've watched so many people struggle with change that I'm not convinced we can change everything we want to change. I'm not convinced that we need, or can find, more self-control or willpower. Maybe we're trying to change the wrong things. Maybe we're setting the wrong goals.

These questions led me to focus more on what to change, what to plan, and what to do with strengths and weaknesses. I started by asking my students a simple, multiple-choice question:

If you want to increase your personal and professional effectiveness, should you:

1. Fix your weaknesses?

2. Build on your strengths?

3. Do both (fix your weaknesses and build on your strengths)?

The overwhelming majority of students chose to both fix weaknesses and build on strengths. This result is consistent with research by Gallup, which indicates that 59 percent of respondents believed that fixing weaknesses was essential to personal development. Only 41 percent chose building strengths as the path to success.[1]

---

1 | "Go Put Your Strengths to Work," Leading Home Care, October 10, 2007, http://leadinghomecare.com/go-put-your-strengths-to-work/.

In the Gallup study, "doing both" wasn't offered as an option. However, I suspect that offering people the option of doing both would have drastically decreased the number of those who chose to build on their strengths.

In my class, I followed up by asking students to support their choice. Why did they choose their answers? It is interesting to explore their rationale for each answer.

Students who chose to fix their weaknesses gave the following reasons:

➜ I'll turn my weaknesses into strengths, and then I'll be even stronger.

➜ You don't need to build on strengths, because they will always be there. They are natural. You don't have to maintain them.

➜ Nobody is perfect. There is always room for improvement.

➜ You are only as strong as your weakest link.

➜ I can think of more weaknesses than strengths.

➜ Weaknesses make you look bad. Managers, coworkers, and others notice your weaknesses and use them against you.

Students who chose to both fix weaknesses *and* build strengths offered similar reasons:

➜ It is important to be well-rounded and balanced.

→ You can't ignore your weaknesses,
because they will trip you up.

→ It is easier to be balanced than great. It is hard to
be so good that your weaknesses are irrelevant.

→ You should work on as many things as you can.

→ There is always room for improvement.

Students who chose to build on strengths believe the following:

→ You can't be good at everything.

→ There is a place for everyone.

→ Nobody is perfect. You'll always have
weaknesses, so don't worry about them.

→ Our weaknesses make us human.

→ It is important to see the best in people
and bring out the best in others.

→ Strengths make up for our weaknesses. A
good offense makes up for a bad defense.

→ It is more enjoyable to build on strengths.

→ Strengths are where you have the greatest
chance of becoming exceptional.

As you can see, there are many different reasons supporting each
approach. The validity of these beliefs and the effectiveness of each
will be explored throughout the rest of the book. For now, it is
enough to note that the beliefs that support fixing weaknesses are

significantly different from the beliefs that only support building on strengths.

It might be helpful at this point to note the responses that best fit your current belief system. How would you respond to the one-question quiz? Why?

The Freak Factor Survey

I wanted to get a better sense of people's beliefs about strengths, weaknesses, and career development, so I created my own survey. The results confirmed my experience in the classroom. Overall, 48 percent of respondents believe that they need to fit in, fix weaknesses, and be well-rounded in order to succeed in their careers. The detailed survey results were as follows:

→ 50 percent agreed and only 35 percent disagreed with the statement, "It is important to fit in at work."*

→ 52 percent agreed and only 35 percent disagreed with the statement, "If I want to improve, I need to fix my weaknesses."

→ 52 percent agreed and only 33 percent disagreed with the statement, "It is important to be well-rounded, especially at work."

→ 52 percent agreed and only 30 percent disagreed with the statement, "I should fix my weaknesses and build my strengths."

➜ 56 percent agreed and only 26 percent disagreed with the statement, "A well-balanced set of characteristics will make me more marketable."

➜ Nearly 25 percent responded "not sure" to "Being different and sticking out will help me in my career."

The agree/disagree percentages don't equal 100, because some respondents chose "not sure."

The results of this survey are important because our beliefs have a profound influence on our actions. Furthermore, the validity of those beliefs has a major influence on the effectiveness of our actions. If we believe the wrong things, then our actions will be ineffective and self-defeating. If we believe the right things, then our actions have the potential to be fruitful and fulfilling.

What Color Are Your Eyes?

The power of our beliefs is illustrated painfully and beautifully by the story of an elementary school teacher in Iowa. In April 1968, Jane Elliott taught her third-grade students an important lesson. She divided the class into two groups based on eye color. The children were then told that blue-eyed children were smarter, kinder, and cleaner than brown-eyed children. Because of this, blue-eyed children were given extra privileges in the classroom. For example, they were allowed to be first in line and got a longer recess.

Brown-eyed children had to wear special collars that designated them as inferior, and throughout the day, their actions were consistently criticized by Elliott. As the day progressed, the supposedly superior blue-eyed children began to tease and insult those with the inferior eye color. Because of this treatment, the inferior children became withdrawn and sad. They also exhibited decreased participation in class activities. In discussions with Elliott, the brown-eyed children admitted that they were indeed less intelligent than their blue-eyed classmates. Their test results and other schoolwork for the day showed a marked decrease in performance.

The next day, Elliott explained to the students that she had made a mistake. The brown-eyed children were actually superior to the blue-eyed ones. The response to this announcement was immediate and profound. The brown-eyed children began to celebrate, while the blue-eyed children became despondent. As happened the day before, the newly superior children began to criticize their supposedly inferior counterparts. The inferior children showed a significant decrease in confidence, energy, and effort, while the apparently superior students demonstrated a commensurate increase in positive attitude, engaged activity, and overall success.

Elliott used this exercise to teach her students about discrimination. It was shortly after the assassination of Martin Luther King Jr., and her students lived in Riceville, Iowa—an all-white community of just under a thousand people. She wanted to help them understand the insidious nature of prejudice and stereotypes. She did this when she chose "a physical characteristic over which they had no control and attributed negative elements to this characteristic."

It is obvious to external observers, especially adults, that there is no real advantage to having a particular eye color. The apparent superiority of the blue-eyed or brown-eyed students was just an illusion. It wasn't real. It was just an exercise. However, the belief that one eye color was good and the other was bad had a major impact on students' behaviors and performance.

Elliott's exercise illustrates the power of our thoughts in determining how we act. More important, it illustrates the incredible change that takes place when we discover that what we thought was bad is actually good or that what we thought was a weakness is actually a strength. Imagine the response of the brown-eyed students when, after a day of humiliation and criticism, the teacher announced that they weren't inferior. Imagine their joy and excitement. Imagine their transformation.

What if what you thought was bad turned out to be good instead? What if your apparent weaknesses were actually strengths? What if the people who have been criticizing you were wrong? What if your teachers, bosses, coworkers, and spouse had all made mistakes? How would you feel? What would you do?

I think that we all experience some form of Elliott's exercise every day. There are three stages to this process: First, other people take a characteristic over which we have "no control" and "attribute negative elements to it." Second, we believe that the criticism is true. We listen to other people's charges and take them to heart. Third, we feel bad. We wish we could change. We vow to turn things around. We promise to do better, but we can't. Gradually, as it did with Elliott's students, frustration begins to erode our happiness and reduce our performance.

It doesn't have to be this way.

**IT'S NEVER TOO LATE TO BE WHO
YOU MIGHT HAVE BEEN.**

—George Eliot

New Beliefs

There are two lies that lead to frustration and failure in our lives. The first lie is that being normal, following the rules, and fitting in will help you succeed. The second lie is that fixing your weaknesses and being balanced and well-rounded is the best route to personal and career fulfillment.

**I JUST FOUND OUT THERE'S NO SUCH THING AS THE
REAL WORLD. JUST A LIE YOU'VE GOT TO RISE ABOVE.**

—John Mayer, *No Such Thing*

We need to replace these self-defeating beliefs with a pair of more accurate and useful assumptions. First, it is good to be different, to stick out, and to be a freak. Second, it is good to flaunt your weaknesses, instead of fixing them. It is good to be unbalanced.

In other words, what makes us weird also makes us wonderful. What makes us weak also makes us strong.

CONFORMITY IS THE RUIN OF THE MIND.

—Jesse Shelley

Most People

Chris Guillebeau's book *The Art of Non-Conformity* argues that "you don't have to live your life the way other people expect you to." Unfortunately, we tend to adjust our behavior based on what most people do. This seems to be human nature, and psychologists refer to it as *social proof.* We believe that if most people are doing something, then it must be a good idea. Unfortunately, this isn't true. Here's where people tend to fall:

→ **Most people are employees.**[2]

→ **Most people (52 percent) don't like their work.**[3]

→ **Most people only have a high school education.**[4]

→ **Most people are in debt.**[5]

→ **Most people make less than $55,000 per year.**[6]

→ **Most people don't exercise regularly.**[7]

2 | Elaine Pofeldt, "U.S. Entrepreneurship Hits Record High," Forbes, May 27, 2013, http://www.forbes.com/sites/elainepofeldt/2013/05/27/u-s-entrepreneurship-hits-record-high/

3 | Susan Adams, "Most Americans Are Unhappy at Work," Forbes, June 20, 2014, http://www.forbes.com/sites/susanadams/2014/06/20/most-americans-are-unhappy-at-work/

4 | "Educational Attainment in the United States," Wikipedia, accessed August 12, 2015, https://en.wikipedia.org/wiki/Educational_attainment_in_the_United_States

5 | Christine DiGangi, "A Whopping 80 Percent of American Are in Debt," MSN, August 3, 2015, http://www.msn.com/en-us/money/personalfinance/a-whopping-80-percent-of-americans-are-in-debt/ar-BBIlyhK

6 | "Household Income in the United States," Wikipedia, accessed August 12, 2015, https://en.wikipedia.org/wiki/Household_income_in_the_United_States

7 | Ryan Jaslow, "CDC: 80 Percent of American Adults Don't Get Recommended Exercise," CBS News, May 3, 2013, http://www.cbsnews.com/news/cdc-80-percent-of-american-adults-dont-get-recommended-exercise/

→ Most people (59 percent) think they'll succeed by fixing their weaknesses.[8]

→ A select few (13 percent) start their own businesses.[2]

→ A select few do what they love.[3]

→ A select few (32 percent) graduate from college.[4]

→ A select few are debt-free.[5]

→ A select few (20 percent) earn a six-figure income. [9]

→ A select few exercise regularly.[7]

→ A select few flaunt their weaknesses, instead of trying to fix them.

I'm not arguing that starting a business, having a college degree, or earning a lot of money are the most important things in life. My point is that you probably don't want what most people have; you probably want what only a select few have. But if you do what most people do, then you probably won't have the life that you want. Nonconformity is important, because you probably want to be like a select few instead of ending up like most people.

8 | "Go Put Your Strengths to Work," Leading Home Care, October 10, 2007, http://leadinghomecare.com/go-put-your-strengths-to-work/

9 | Craig Guillot, "$100,000 Income: No Big Deal Anymore," Bankrate.com, last updated January 8, 2015, http://www.bankrate.com/finance/personal-finance/100-000-income-no-big-deal-anymore-1.aspx

**I'M NOT GOING TO CHANGE THE WAY I
LOOK OR THE WAY I FEEL TO CONFORM TO
ANYTHING. I'VE ALWAYS BEEN A FREAK.**

—John Lennon

Differentiation

After a speaking engagement in Boston, I was doing some shopping and saw a sign for sale in a small store. It read, "I think the only normal people are the ones you don't know too well." This is important. There is no such thing as normal. We only imagine that other people are normal. Similarly, other people know that they aren't normal but assume that we are.

Even if it was good to be normal, it isn't possible. No one is normal. Normal is just an abstract concept that doesn't exist in reality.

A lot of people pay lip service to the value of being different. An essential marketing strategy for most organizations includes differentiation. However, it is difficult to be different. When others notice that you are different, they try to make you fit in.

In his book *Deep Change*, Robert Quinn argues that "deviance will always generate external pressures to conform … If you perform beyond the norms, the systems will adjust and try to make you normal." Einstein put it more strongly when he said, "Great spirits have always experienced violent opposition from mediocre minds."

Some people will always see deviance as wrong and dangerous, so they respond with disdain and mockery. That is why e. e. cummings warned, "It takes courage to grow up and turn out to be who you really are." It can be risky to stick out. Because of this, we tend to give up on being who we really are, and instead, we just do what other people are doing.

We want to fit in. We don't want to be different or unusual. We don't want to stick out. It seems safe to be normal. Why risk "violent opposition?"

However, it can be just as dangerous to simply remain average. Management guru Tom Peters argues that "the White Collar Revolution will wipe out indistinct workers and reward the daylights out of those with True Distinction." He believes that it is no longer safe to be the same, to be normal—to be indistinct. Let that sink in for a minute. He is saying that the only safe move, the only prudent choice, the only wise decision is to become a freak—to be unusual, different, strange, and remarkable.

READ, EVERY DAY, SOMETHING NO ONE ELSE IS READING ... IT IS BAD FOR THE MIND TO BE ALWAYS PART OF UNANIMITY.

—Christopher Morley

But is Peters's advice realistic? To answer that question, let's take a look at Warren Buffet, one of the richest and most generous people in the world. Buffet explained his formula for success in a *New York Times* article written during the spectacular meltdown of the financial sector in 2008: "Be fearful when others are greedy, and be greedy when others are fearful." In other words, his formula for success is to do the opposite of what everyone else is doing. He's different. He's a deviant.

Michael Lewis wrote *The Big Short* to tell the story of the few people who predicted and prepared for the crash of the subprime mortgage industry. One of the people Lewis profiled was Mike Burry, a neurologist in California who has Asperger's syndrome (a form of autism). Burry's investment company, Scion Capital, had returns of 490 percent from 2000 to 2008; the Standard & Poor's 500 returned only 2 percent during that same period.

Burry foresaw the demise of the real estate sector as early as 2005, and he made nearly a billion dollars when it imploded. When asked to explain his special insight and willingness to go against the grain, he credited his success to the example of Warren Buffet. Burry believes that Buffet's life proves that "to succeed in a spectacular fashion you have to be spectacularly unusual." We miss out on spectacular success when we are unwilling to be spectacularly unusual.

DON'T TRY TO STAND OUT FROM THE CROWD. AVOID CROWDS ALTOGETHER.

—Hugh MacLeod, *gapingvoid*

Seven Reasons to Be Different

1. Being different makes you **rare**.
    Being normal makes you **ordinary**.

Scarcity increases value. Diamonds are valuable primarily because they are rare. Sand and salt are far less valuable, not because they aren't useful but because they are so ordinary and plentiful.

I'M THE BOSS. I DON'T MAKE COPIES. I MAKE ORIGINALS.

—Michael Scott, *The Office*

2. Being different makes you **original**.
Being normal makes you easy to **imitate**.

One reason that many jobs are outsourced or computerized is that they've become so routine that they are easy to automate and simple for others to learn and duplicate. In his book *Never Eat Alone,* Keith Ferrazzi argues that we must "be distinct or be extinct … The best brands, like the most interesting people, have a distinct message … When it comes to making an impression, differentiation is the name of the game. Confound expectation. Shake it up. How? There's one guaranteed way to stand out in the professional world. Be yourself."

In his blog post "The Five Laws of Being an Interesting Brand," personal branding expert Dan Schawbel writes, "Be yourself. Your personality is your best and most distinct attribute. I can't copy it, nor can any of my readers or anyone else in the world. It's easy to not be yourself sometimes because you want to impress someone or you want to fit in with cultural or group norms. When you start acting like everyone else, you lose the essence and beauty that would actually make people interested in you. By being yourself, you're bound to appeal to certain types of people."

3. Being different makes you **noticeable**.
   Being normal makes you **invisible**.

Fitting in makes us invisible. If we do things well, no one can see us. If we fit in at work, we don't get in trouble. We don't get fired, but we don't get promoted, either. We don't get interesting projects, and we don't get challenging tasks.

If our business fits in, everyone drives right by. No one stops. They don't know we're even there. If they do stop, they don't stay long and don't buy anything because our products or services are just like everyone else's. If we fit in, we don't get any attention. And attention is one of the most valuable gifts we can receive from others.

Mark Sanborn is a well-known speaker and author of *The Fred Factor*, a story about an unusual mail carrier. Fred was different than most postal employees. He was so extraordinary that he got Sanborn's attention and ended up as the subject of a best-selling book. Fred's story teaches us an important lesson. As Sanborn said in a recent blog post, "We are bombarded by people and messages every day, all trying to get our attention. With limited attention, there is only so much we can give." People only take notice when something is unusual or surprising.

4. Being different makes you **surprising**.
   Being normal makes you **predictable**.

I was walking down the street in San Francisco and saw a homeless man with a cardboard sign, the kind that usually says "Will Work for Food" or "Homeless. Please Help." But this one didn't say anything predictable. It said, "Who Am I Kidding? It's Miller Time!" As the Heath brothers explain in *Made to Stick*, we are more likely to be persuaded by messages that are unexpected.

5. Being different makes you **memorable**.
   Being normal makes you **forgettable**.

We remember the unusual events in our lives, not the common ones. If no one remembers you or your message, then you don't have the opportunity to influence them. The worst criticism that Simon Cowell, the caustic judge on *American Idol*, can give is that a contestant is forgettable. In contrast, one of his most powerful compliments is that a contestant is memorable. He recently told one girl, "You are such a strange person. I mean that as a compliment." We remember people who are strange.

6. Being different makes you **remarkable**. Being normal gives people **nothing to talk about.**

   When we see something different, we want to tell other people about it. Once people remember you, the biggest challenge is getting them to tell others about you. As Mark Sanborn demonstrated, if you are remarkable enough, someone might even write a book about you. Matt Langdon collects stories of everyday heroes and posts them on his blog. This word of mouth is powerful for individuals and businesses.

7. Being different makes you **influential**. Being normal makes you **powerless**.

   If other people are sharing your message, it increases your influence because it enables you to reach a larger audience.

What Makes You Rare?

Being a freak is about being different, unusual, uncommon, and rare. At this point, it might be helpful to think about what makes you odd, atypical, and exceptional. We tend to focus on the ways in which we are similar to others. We want to be normal, and we emphasize the characteristics that help us to fit in with everyone else. However, as we just discussed, this approach isn't very effective.

What is it about you that makes you different from most people? Here is my list:

→ At a height of 6'6", I'm taller than 99 percent of people in the world. My tall stature might also contribute to greater reproductive success.

→ I suffer from Morton's toe, meaning that my second toe is longer than my first. Only 10 percent of the world's population has this condition.

→ I've completed a marathon, a feat accomplished by only 0.1 percent of Americans.

→ I'm the father of three daughters and no sons. I can't find the exact statistics on this, but apparently it increases my risk of getting prostate cancer, wearing nail polish, and watching Strawberry Shortcake cartoons.

→ I have a very small neck: 14.5 inches in circumference. I know that this is unusual because I can't buy shirts with that size neck hole with the proper sleeve length at traditional stores. I have to buy my clothes online. The good news is that my skinny neck decreases my risk for heart disease and sleep apnea.

→ I earned a doctor of management degree. Thirty-two percent of Americans have graduated from college, 12 percent have graduate degrees, and just 3 percent have doctorates.[10]

10 | "Educational Attainment in the United States," Wikipedia, accessed August 12, 2015, https://en.wikipedia.org/wiki/Educational_attainment_in_the_United_States

➜ I'm a nerd. I listen to and read about fifty books per year. My record is one hundred. Most people don't do this: the average is four books per year. Twenty-seven percent don't read any books. Many of my fellow nerds are also older and female.

➜ I'm self-employed. This is unusual. Most people are employees. Depending on which report you look at, self-employed people make up less than 15 percent of the workforce.

What about you? What makes you rare? You can use the space below to create your list. You might find distinctiveness in your appearance, personality, habits, accomplishments, career, education, and/or family.

_____

_____

_____

_____

_____

_____

_____

_____

_____

A Bad Kid

I haven't always been proud of my strangeness. For most of my life I was unhappy because I couldn't fit in, wasn't well-rounded, and couldn't conquer my weaknesses. So how did I find my own freak factor? How did I find the courage to be different?

I was a bad kid—at least, that's what everyone told me. My parents and teachers had three primary goals during my entire childhood. They wanted me to sit down, be quiet, and do what I was told. My inability to master these basic skills was a major problem, especially since I was forced to spend most of my childhood in school, sitting still, listening, and following instructions (or at least trying to). Because of my weaknesses, I was told repeatedly that I was obnoxious and immature, had a bad attitude, and lacked self-control. Even my parents called me "motormouth" because of my nonstop chatter.

You can only hear people tell you something is wrong with you for so long before you begin to believe them. I saw myself as immature, out of control, rebellious, hyperactive, and unattractive, because others saw me that way. This didn't give me a lot of hope for my future, and the problems continued throughout high school and into college. I did well for a while, early in my career, but soon my distaste for authority, my hyperactivity, and my consistent failure to keep quiet began haunting me again.

"This isn't working out," said Camille, my boss. "The problem is that you're just not a team player." Hearing this made me sick to my stomach. I was only a few weeks into my new job at a large nonprofit in Chicago. My former employer had recently merged with another organization, and I went from working mostly alone in a two-person operation to working with hundreds of people on a five-person team.

Now I was sitting in a booth at McDonald's with my boss and two coworkers. They'd called this meeting to inform me that I needed to make some major changes in order to succeed in my new role. I was stunned. I had been very successful in my two previous jobs, both of which required me to work independently. This was my biggest strength, and I had thought that it would serve me well in my new position. But I was wrong.

It seemed like everything that was good about me was working against me. The very trait that my last boss praised me for, my ability to work independently, was about to cost me my job. My new coworkers saw me as a lone ranger. They complained that I didn't ask for their input and that I talked too much, too often, and for too long in meetings. I didn't seem open to their involvement. Their organization valued teamwork very highly, and if I couldn't change, they would ask me to leave.

Seeing the writing on the wall, I started looking for something new. I found a job in a city closer to my family, but I was soon confronted with new challenges. My new responsibilities required me to create a brand-new business within an existing company. It was a perfect fit, because I got to develop a plan for a dramatic change within the organization. The plan required a major investment of capital and created a lot of positive visibility for me and my company. After the new operation was in place, I was promoted to a senior management position and immediately began talking to my boss, the organization's CEO, about other projects.

However, there was a conflict between my interest in starting new projects and the company's need for me to manage ongoing operations. There was also a conflict between my desire for rapid change and my boss's patient and deliberate approach. Our meetings gradually became more and more contentious: my boss continually admonished me to slow down and focus on improving existing processes, and I argued for the need to speed up and dramatically transform the entire organization.

I strongly believed that I could do a better job of running the company. It was very difficult for me to follow someone with such a dramatically different approach. I'd never been very good at doing what I was told, and I strongly valued freedom and the opportunity to control my own future.

Additionally, it was clear that some of my employees wanted me to provide more structure and specific direction. I was always talking about vision, mission, values, and the long-term goals of my division, but I devoted little time to offering detailed instructions regarding short-term goals and daily activities. I believed that it was important to provide my employees with the autonomy to make these decisions. I thought that they had more insight into these issues than I did, since they were on the front lines every day.

Meetings were still a problem as well. I'm very intuitive and seemed to instantly develop strong feelings about how the organization should proceed. Unfortunately, I couldn't always clearly articulate why I felt the way I did, and I didn't necessarily present concrete evidence for the effectiveness of my recommendations. But this didn't keep me from sharing my ideas very passionately and arguing for them strongly against challenges from others on the management team.

These issues began to take a toll on my health and happiness. I was constantly frustrated and irritable. I became very self-conscious and lost my confidence. My weight began to balloon as my eating habits and sleep patterns deteriorated. Every day at work was a battle, and I began to dread going into the office. I couldn't understand how my past success had turned into such a mess.

Eventually I resigned, but even that went badly. I was asked to leave before my chosen resignation date because my boss and subordinates felt that I was no longer committed to the organization.

In summary, I had these weaknesses:

→ I was too talkative and wasn't a good listener.

→ I was hyperactive and wasn't able to sit still.

→ I was too independent and wasn't a team player.

→ I was too intuitive and wasn't rational enough.

→ I was too passionate and wasn't calm enough.

→ I was too strategic and wasn't operational enough.

→ I was too focused on the future and wasn't focused enough on the present.

→ I was too impulsive and wasn't patient enough.

These seem like substantial challenges, and a traditional approach to personal development would focus on fixing these weaknesses. However, I chose a different approach. I didn't improve by overcoming my weaknesses. I didn't really change myself at all. I succeeded by flaunting my weaknesses and finding situations that valued the positive side of my apparent flaws.

Instead of changing myself, I changed my situation. I quit my job as a manager and began working as a college professor. This change allowed me to teach two of my favorite subjects: strategy and managing change. I also started my own business, helping companies with strategic planning. My clients appreciated my strategic thinking and ability to help them see the big picture. They didn't need me to be detail oriented and focused on operations—they had that covered. They needed me to help them look to the future and identify the larger issues that their organizations were facing.

Then, I gradually transitioned from consulting to training to professional speaking. As a keynote speaker, I get praised for my energy and enthusiasm. My passion is infectious and helps me connect with audiences. As a solo entrepreneur, I can change quickly and act on my intuition without having to convince others to follow. I can also work independently and don't need to be a team player. My initiative and obsession with achievement keeps me motivated without direction or supervision from others. I'm in control, and I love it.

I'm rarely criticized anymore for my weaknesses. I still have all the same flaws; they just don't matter in my new work. I've lost weight and started running marathons, ultramarathons, and triathlons. I feel energized and confident. My work provides me with happiness, fulfillment, and a sense that I have truly found my calling.

It is important to note that I was fortunate to have one person along the way who saw the strengths hiding inside my weaknesses. Late in my sophomore year of college, Elliott Anderson (the resident director of the men's dorm) approached me and asked me to apply for a resident assistant position. This was a big surprise. Up to this point, I had thought that I was the reason that the college employed resident assistants. I saw myself as a rule breaker, not a member of the enforcement team. However, Elliott saw something else.

Elliott saw a lot of himself when he looked at me. He was also a bad kid who turned out okay. He thought that maybe he could help me. It was great to work with him, and we are still friends today. He was the first one to call me "freak," which is one of the few nicknames I am proud of, and was the inspiration for the title of this book.

My unlikely transformation illustrates the seven strategies for finding your freak factor:

1. **Awareness**—Identify your strengths and weaknesses.

2. **Acceptance**—Stop trying to fix your weaknesses.

3. **Appreciation**—Embrace your unique characteristics.

4. **Amplification**—Flaunt your weaknesses.

5. **Alignment**—Find the right fit.

6. **Avoidance**—Move out of situations that highlight your weaknesses.

7. **Affiliation**—Partner with people who are strong where you are weak.

FREAK PROFILE: Mary Mack

Mary contacted me after reading an early electronic version of *The Freak Factor*. Her boss gave it to her, and Mary liked what she read so much that she decided to quit her job. That's probably not the response her boss was hoping for.

Mary now works as a personal trainer and specialty fitness instructor in Minneapolis, Minnesota. She is also a healthy-life-style blogger. When she's not training clients, she volunteers with Bolder Options, a youth mentorship program in Minneapolis. She just ran her first marathon in Honolulu. Here is the rest of her story:

> I have always colored outside the lines. As a child, I struggled with the confines of a classroom, with doing work and with having to fit into any kind of mold, except for the one I made myself. But when I graduated from college, I fell into a job, at an office, in a cubicle. I felt important, adult, professional, like I was doing what I should do.
>
> Years passed and I moved from one office to the next, from one set of gray walls to the next. I made slight advances, as much as a literature major in Corporate America can. I kept changing titles but always kept "assistant" on the end, like a tag line. I was excelling at being mediocre. I was barely getting by, lacking in joy and feeling inadequate.

The problem wasn't just the jobs I was working, but also my performance in them.

What was wrong with me? I was a smart, passionate and vibrant free-thinker and I could screw up an office supply order with the best of them. Then I found something that I really could do well—working a front desk, greeting people, and being the face of a company! I excelled. I was given more responsibility and started to struggle with the expectations. I started to examine the things I fell short on, the projects that I procrastinated on, the tasks that I screwed up.

Did I have ADD? ADHD? Did I have a bad attitude?

But the woman I worked for saw my full potential. One time, when talking about a certain project, she asked me, "Who told you that you weren't capable?" Then she handed me a copy of *The Freak Factor*. What I read changed the way that I looked at myself and my work.

If you are anything like me then you probably have an idea of what your weakness are. As much as I wish I had fewer weaknesses, I don't really intend to go through life sweeping them under the rug or making excuses for them like I had been up to that point. I learned to look at my weakness a little differently after reading *The Freak Factor.*

Most people focus on their weaknesses and work hard on turning them into strengths. I was working hard trying to improve where I fell short, trying to find fixes and shortcuts and ways to work better. For a while, it worked. Things got a little better, but I was hammering my weakness into submission only to end up with a slightly dented version of the original product.

The main key to succeeding by finding the strengths hiding inside your weaknesses is to seek out situations where you can use your strengths and excel there. If you are constantly in situations where you are required to use your weaknesses you will not feel like you are succeeding. When you feel that, examine the situation and ask "Why don't I feel successful here?" You will be able to pinpoint corresponding strengths more easily when you see your weaknesses for what they are.

I learned to choose situations that fit my natural strengths. That meant a career change. I researched becoming a personal trainer, did the work, and leaped out into a world of the unknown. I moved from a well-paying corporate job, which I was mediocre at, into unpaid internships and a world where I was able to tap into my strengths and use my natural skills to excel.

I have been working as a personal trainer for only eight months and have already been praised by my boss as being a "professional highlight." I've been encouraged to never lose my natural love and enthusiasm for people and training. I've also received countless positive comments.

I was so excited about Mary's transformation that I wanted to learn more. The following are her answers to a few of my follow-up questions.

Can you tell me more about particular weaknesses and how you discovered the strengths that corresponded with them?

I was never built to sit still. As a receptionist, I was always confined to a front desk and copy room. I felt restless and agitated, and that made me feel unproductive. I actually was unproductive, too. I would start projects, get bored, and leave them half-done. It wasn't that I was bored with the project itself; I was bored with my inability to move around in my position and bored with the confinement of my job. I would have multiple projects half-completed and no motivation to finish any of them.

Weaknesses that I discovered on that job were only weaknesses within that environment. In a different setting, they could easily be strengths. For instance, when someone would request a project or special order from me, I would just dive right in and have to backpedal later. In hindsight, I can see the value in asking all the important questions up front, but my enthusiastic drive was never tapped into the way it is in some of my current ventures.

What weaknesses did you struggle with on the job?

I had to work extra hard to be organized in the way that the rest of the team required. There was little room for individual style in my work. As a personal trainer, I still have to do paperwork, like tracking client progress, planning sessions, follow-up, and notes. The difference is that I am free to do it on my own time and in my own way. It's a much more creative environment.

What is it about being a trainer that matches your unique strengths?

One of my strengths is that I have a heart for serving and helping people. I'm also good at showing people how to do things in the best way. I'm a natural leader and planner, but due to some situations in life, I adopted more of a follower approach. Sitting behind a desk as a receptionist or in a cube kept me from being able to lead. I may have been the face of the organization, but I didn't have the opportunity to lead or use the true power that I knew I had. My strength was never in administrative duties. I excelled much more in the personal and social aspects. Now, as a trainer, I have the opportunity to lead and direct individuals and groups.

1. AWARENESS

· ·

**WE ARE LED TO TRUTH BY OUR WEAKNESSES
AS WELL AS OUR STRENGTHS.**

—Parker Palmer, *Let Your Life Speak*

The goals of this chapter are to define a few key terms and to help you identify your unique strengths and weaknesses.

Freak

The July 2008 cover of *Sports Illustrated* simply said "The Freak" next to a picture of Tim Lincecum, a pitcher for the San Francisco Giants. The magazine called him a freak because he is just 5'10" and weighs only 170 pounds. In contrast, the average pitcher in Major League Baseball is over six feet tall and weighs closer to 200 pounds. Lincecum isn't normal. As Mike Powell explains, "The normal stride length for a pitcher is 77% to 87% of his height. Lincecum's stride is 129%, or roughly 7.5 feet."

Tim's father, Chris, wasn't particularly excited about his son being called a freak and called Tim to talk about it.

"Tim, everybody is calling you a freak."

"Well, Dad, I am. Why?"

"How can you say you're a freak? You're just a good athlete."

"Okay, is Michael Jordan a freak? Tiger Woods? Jack Nicklaus?"

"Yeah, I'd consider them freaks," Chris said. "Then, okay, you're a freak."

However, not everyone is excited about working with freaks. A lot of teams refused to draft Lincecum because of his unusual stature and unconventional pitching style. "One guy (a scout) said his mechanics were unorthodox, and people ran with it." It was their loss.

The freak won the Cy Young Award in 2008 and 2009. The next time Lincecum was on the cover of *Sports Illustrated* was two years later, in the final issue of 2010. The headline was "Get Your Freak On," and he was pictured celebrating the Giants' World Series victory, in which the little guy with the weird delivery had won two games.

Tim Lincecum is an interesting example, but what exactly does it mean to be a freak?

The term *freak* can mean maniac; fanatic; something unusual, irregular, or abnormally formed; an eccentric or nonconformist person; or a person who is obsessed with something.

In this book I define a freak as a person who is unique because of a natural, positive obsession. I use the word as a compliment. However, being a freak wasn't always considered a good thing.

SIGN SAYS LONG-HAIRED FREAKY PEOPLE NEED NOT APPLY.

—Five Man Electrical Band, "Signs"

The *Wikipedia* entry for *freak* explains that "a freak is often considered a pejorative term for an organism with an abnormality of some kind. The older usage, referring to the physically deformed, such as that would be seen in a sideshow, has generally fallen into disuse." Notice that *freak* used to be a negative label. I purposely chose the term because of its history and ambiguous meaning.

Unique

"In current usage, the word freak denotes a person with an unusual personality." This meaning is consistent with my use of the word. As we discussed previously, being a freak means being different.

Unfortunately, instead of embracing our uniqueness, we often try to hide it in an effort to be more normal. We do so because many people discourage our uniqueness by framing it as a weakness. That leads us to the next part of the definition.

"The word is still used when describing mutations in plants and animals but more often is applied to humans." I think the idea of mutation is also a helpful one. Mutants are weird, strange, and bizarre.

"A freak can be formally defined as someone not falling within typical standard deviations. For example, people of small stature would not be classified as freaks unless they are within the third standard deviation for the general population, while the same principle would apply to exceptionally tall people." I like the final part of the definition because, as an "exceptionally tall" person, it officially classifies me as a freak.

Positive

"The word freak, when used in a slang context, also has positive connotations. The term can be used to describe one who is unusually skilled or talented in a particular area."

This is my favorite part. I intend to use freak in a positive way. I think it is good to be a freak, and I want to encourage you to feel the same way. Who wouldn't want to be "unusually skilled or talented?"

Obsession

"Freak can also mean someone who is utterly obsessed with…a particular activity."

Steve Almond is a fellow ectomorph and the author of *Candyfreak*, a hilarious and fascinating book about his obsession with candy. In the book, Almond describes his travels across the country, exploring the inner workings of famous and obscure purveyors of sweet delights. His book and his life definitely illustrate the positive aspects of obsession. Despite the fact that his obsession is candy, he is very philosophical. He thinks of *freak* as a verb: an active desire.

"We don't choose our freaks. They choose us … We may not understand why we freak on a particular food or band or sports team. We may have no conscious control over our allegiances. But they arise from our most sacred fears and desires, and, as such they represent the truest expression of our selves." When you read Almond's descriptions of his experiences with candy, you can feel his unrestrained passion, and you almost start to feel the same way.

Almond illustrates the positive elements of obsession. His writing makes it obvious that he has embraced his freakiness, and he flaunts it on each and every page. For example, one section discusses candy porn, and another explores his oral fixation.

Despite his constant candy consumption, Almond is able to maintain a slim physique. This is due to his ectomorph body type. Steve has found a great fit between his addiction and his natural build.

Natural

Freaks "can be classified into two groups: *natural freaks* and *made freaks*. A *natural freak* would usually refer to a genetic abnormality, while a *made freak* is a once normal person who experienced or initiated an alteration at some point in life."

The goal of this book is to help you discover and enhance your natural freakiness. I don't think any of us are, or were, normal, and most of us don't have to go to the trouble of making ourselves into freaks. We just came that way. As Almond said, "We don't choose our freaks, they choose us." I hope this book will help you to accept and appreciate your innate qualities.

The idea of a "made" freak is also helpful. I'd like to help you make yourself into a bigger freak than you already are. As Marcus Buckingham says in his book *First, Break All the Rules*, "Don't try to put in what was left out, try to draw out what was left in." This sentiment is echoed by Tom Rath of the Gallup organization. He believes that "you can't be anything you want to be, but you can be more of who you are." That really sums up the purpose of this book: to help you to become more of who you are so that you can help others to do the same.

Strength

While we're defining terms, it is probably important to clarify the meanings of the terms *strength* and *weakness*. Gallup is the leader of the *strengths revolution*, which is an application of positive psychology to individual and organizational performance. Gallup defines *strength* as "the ability to consistently produce a nearly perfect positive outcome in a specific task." This is a good definition, but it is too specific for our purposes.

Gallup's definition of *talent* is closer to what I mean by *strength*. In *Now, Discover Your Strengths*, coauthors Marcus Buckingham and Donald Clifton describe talents as "a recurring pattern of thought, feeling or behavior that can be productively applied." When I talk about strengths in this book, this is what I mean.

I define *strength* as a pattern of passion and proficiency. Strengths are patterns because they describe how we usually, consistently, or regularly feel or act. Strengths aren't things that we sometimes do, occasionally like, or rarely experience. This is like the difference between a solitary action and a habit. Actions are isolated events, while habits are patterns.

Having *passion* means that you love something. You can't wait for activities that allow you to exercise your strengths, and you are energized by participating in those activities. Too often, self-improvement programs focus on perseverance and discipline while neglecting passion. However, a basic understanding of human nature shows us that people do what makes them feel good and avoid actions that make them feel bad. This is why the "no pain, no gain" philosophy leads to so much frustration.

I believe that passion creates perseverance. We dedicate ourselves to those things that we enjoy and that make us feel good. Those positive emotions carry us through times of potential difficulty or struggle. I don't think that many people successfully persevere and accomplish goals that they don't want to or engage in activities that they don't like.

Proficiency means that you have a talent in an area. You are good at it. You have had success in the past, and you anticipate success in the future.

Ability is essential to motivation. According to expectancy theory, we will not be motivated to do something unless we can answer yes to each of the following three questions:

1. Can I do it?

2. Will I be rewarded?

3. Do I value the reward?

Notice the first question. If you don't think that you can do something, it doesn't matter what rewards are offered. Motivation requires ability (or at least the perception that you have the ability). However, ability and proficiency aren't the same as perfection. There are always opportunities to build on our strengths, and this is not the same as fixing a weakness.

Weakness

I define *weakness* as a pattern of apathy, aversion, or failure. Each of these words is important. We've already discussed the definition of a pattern. *Apathy* means that you have no interest in an area.

You don't necessarily dislike it; you just don't care. *Aversion*, on the other hand, means that you find an activity boring or unpleasant. Weaknesses usually drain us. We become exhausted when forced to do things in our areas of weakness.

Failure means that you have a lack of ability and have consistently struggled with something in the past. As we'll discuss later, the presence of apathy, aversion, or failure is enough to create a weakness, since any one of these is enough to limit your potential for success.

LEARN WHAT YOU ARE AND BE SUCH.

—Pindar

Self-Awareness

I'm not a huge *American Idol* fan. I enjoy the first few episodes of a season, where some really bad singers are allowed to audition, but then my interest fades. However, besides the entertainment value of some of these dreadful performances, we can also learn important lessons from the tone-deaf contestants.

Many motivational speakers encourage their audience members to "do what you love" and "pursue your passions." That seems like good advice, but it is only the beginning of good advice. Think about it. In order to appear on *American Idol*, a potential contestant has to travel to the host city, wait for hours or days, sometimes in the extreme heat or cold in large stadiums or parking lots, with just a faint hope of even being seen by the judges, much less being selected for the next round.

It is safe to assume that most of these people love music. They love singing, and they are passionate about what they do. Some of them are even trying to fulfill their dreams by singing in bars or restaurants or by teaching music lessons.

Unfortunately, most of them lack talent. They are terrible singers. They have bad voices. It is painful to listen to them, and no amount of passion can overcome those problems.

It is important to know what your strengths and weaknesses are. I am mystified by the lack of self-awareness exhibited by some of these aspiring stars. It isn't that they aren't good enough to be the next American Idol; they are so bad that they shouldn't be allowed to perform on karaoke night at a local bar. If they knew (or were willing to admit) that they lacked the ability to sing well, they could focus on other activities where they had more potential.

This chapter is based on the belief that improving your self-awareness can improve your effectiveness.

Twenty Questions

Below is a list of questions to help you discover your strengths and weaknesses. I encourage you to take some time to consider each of them before moving on to the next section. The following chapters assume that you have a strong awareness of your strengths and weaknesses. Asking yourself these questions will help you develop or improve that awareness:

1. What is the **biggest success** that I've ever had?

2. What was the **happiest day** of my life?
   What was I doing? Who was I with?

3. What was my **favorite class** in school?
   Which part did I like best?

4. What do others **consistently praise me** for?

5. Which activities **energize** me?
   When do I lose track of time?

6. What was my **favorite job**? What did I like about it?

7. What is the **biggest failure** that
   I've ever experienced?

8. What was my **least favorite class** in school?
   Which part did I dislike the most?

9. What do others **consistently criticize** me for?

10. Which activities **drain my energy**?

11. What do I **wish I could change** about myself?

12. On which tasks do I tend to **procrastinate**?

13. What was my **worst job**? What did I hate about it?

14. How can I **build on my strengths**?

15. How can I **flaunt my weaknesses**?
    How can I do more of what people tell
    me not to do? (amplification)

16. How can I **do the opposite** of what
    everyone else is doing? (amplification)

17. How can I work with people who are **strong where I am weak**? (affiliation)

18. What situations **highlight my strengths** and make my weaknesses irrelevant? (alignment)

19. How can I **stick out** instead of trying to fit in?

20. How can I **stop doing** activities that drain me and replace them with those that energize me? (avoidance)

IT'S UP TO EACH OF US ALONE TO FIGURE OUT WHO WE ARE, WHO WE ARE NOT, AND TO ACT MORE OR LESS CONSISTENTLY WITH THOSE CONCLUSIONS.

—Tom Peters

Identifying Your Strengths

1. Put check marks in the boxes to the left
    of your positive characteristics.

2. If you notice any characteristics that are definitely
    not strengths of yours, draw a line through them.

3. Choose your top five strengths, and rank them
    from one to five (one being the strongest).

x	Strengths	Rank
	1. Creative, Innovative	
	2. Organized, Systematic	
	3. Dedicated, Persistent	
	4. Flexible, Adaptable	
	5. Enthusiastic, Passionate	
	6. Calm, Laid-Back	
	7. Dynamic, Active	
	8. Reflective, Thoughtful	
	9. Adventurous, Courageous	
	10. Responsible, Cautious	
	11. Activist, Revolutionary	
	12. Conventional, Traditional	
	13. Direct, Honest	
	14. Polite, Courteous	
	15. Cooperative, Helpful	
	16. Competitive, Assertive	
	17. Theoretical, Idealistic	
	18. Realistic, Practical	
	19. Independent, Self-Sufficient	
	20. Team Player, Unselfish	
	21. Objective, Unbiased	
	22. Sensitive, Caring	

x	Strengths	Rank
	23. Humble, Modest	
	24. Confident, Secure	
	25. Patient, Cautious	
	26. Spontaneous, Instinctive	
	27. Influential, Powerful	
	28. Obedient, Dutiful	
	29. Motivated, Ambitious	
	30. Relaxed, Easygoing	
	31. Analytical, Rational	
	32. Compassionate, Sympathetic	
	33. Positive, Encouraging	
	34. Realistic, Sensible	
	35. Open-Minded, Tolerant	
	36. Certain, Decisive	
	37. Extravagant, Elegant	
	38. Simple, Natural	
	39. Self-Controlled, Disciplined	
	40. Fun, Entertaining	
	41. Serious, Mature	
	42. Funny, Amusing	
	43. Focused, Diligent	
	44. Exploring, Discovering	
	45. Generous, Altruistic	
	46. Frugal, Thrifty	
	47. Curious, Inquisitive	
	48. Content, Satisfied	
	49. Loyal, Devoted	
	50. Adaptable, Flexible	
	51. Detail-Oriented, Meticulous	
	52. Global, General	

Identifying Your Weaknesses

1. Put check marks in the boxes to the left of your negative characteristics.

2. If you notice any characteristics that are definitely not weaknesses of yours, draw a line through them.

3. Choose your top five weaknesses, and rank them from one to five (one being the weakest).

x	Weaknesses	Rank
	1. Chaotic, Disorganized	
	2. Rigid, Inflexible	
	3. Stubborn, Obstinate	
	4. Inconsistent, Unreliable	
	5. Quick-Tempered, Angry	
	6. Unfeeling, Emotionless	
	7. Frantic, Restless	
	8. Quiet, Shy	
	9. Reckless, Irresponsible	
	10. Boring, Uninteresting	
	11. Rebellious, Radical	
	12. Old-Fashioned, Conforming	
	13. Blunt, Rude	
	14. Superficial, Insincere	
	15. Passive, Submissive	
	16. Antagonistic, Aggressive	
	17. Unrealistic, Impractical	
	18. Negative, Critical	
	19. Isolated, Selfish	
	20. Dependent, Needy	
	21. Detached, Insensitive	
	22. Vulnerable, Emotional	

x	Weaknesses	Rank
	23. Timid, Insecure	
	24. Arrogant, Conceited	
	25. Slow, Indecisive	
	26. Impatient, Impulsive	
	27. Controlling, Manipulative	
	28. Weak, Subservient	
	29. Obsessive, Workaholic	
	30. Unmotivated, Lazy	
	31. Critical, Judgmental	
	32. Lenient, Indulgent	
	33. Flattering, Naive	
	34. Negative, Discouraging	
	35. Unprincipled, Naive	
	36. Opinionated, Dogmatic	
	37. Complicated, Difficult	
	38. Plain, Dull	
	39. Harsh, Stiff	
	40. Hedonistic, Self-Indulgent	
	41. Humorless, Solemn	
	42. Silly, Immature	
	43. Limited, Restricted, Narrow	
	44. Distractible, Unfocused	
	45. Pushover, Sucker	
	46. Stingy, Cheap	
	47. Intrusive, Nosy	
	48. Apathetic, Indifferent	
	49. Robotic, Gullible	
	50. Disloyal, Fickle	
	51. Perfectionist, Compulsive	
	52. Sloppy, Careless	

Negativity Bias

Was it easier to identify your strengths or your weaknesses? Did you select more strengths or weaknesses? If you're like most people, you had an easier time identifying your weaknesses, and you listed more weaknesses than strengths. This is because of a psychological phenomenon called the *negativity bias*.

FEW PEOPLE CAN SEE GENIUS IN SOMEONE WHO HAS OFFENDED THEM.

—Robertson Davies

Negativity bias means that we pay more attention to negative experiences and see them as more important and meaningful than positive experiences. We tend to see what's wrong instead of what's right, even if what's wrong is really minor and what's right is really major. In other words, we naturally notice our own weaknesses and have a more difficult time seeing or valuing our strengths.

Everyone has a negativity bias, and that is why other people are more likely to criticize us for our weaknesses instead of praising us for our strengths. Additionally, people even tend to describe others' positive characteristics in a negative way. But we have to remember that others' descriptions aren't correct. They are biased.

HE HAS ALL THE VIRTUES I DISLIKE AND NONE OF THE VICES I ADMIRE.

—Sir Winston Churchill

Fundamental Attribution Error

There is another reason that other people consistently and incorrectly see us as less than we truly are. It seems to be human nature to attribute negative motives and characteristics to others. Social psychologists call this the *fundamental attribution error.*

Specifically, we tend to dismiss situational explanations for others' behavior and believe, instead, that something is inherently wrong with them. For example, if someone is acting nervous in an interview, we usually perceive that he or she is unqualified or has something to hide. The obvious explanation, however, is that the person is nervous because he or she is in an interview. The situation, not someone's personal characteristics, is likely the cause of the anxiety.

This almost unavoidable error is another reason why other people consistently focus on our weaknesses and fail to detect our strengths. Unfortunately, we don't recognize this and begin to believe what other people tell us about ourselves.

> NATURE NEVER REPEATS HERSELF, AND
> THE POSSIBILITIES OF ONE HUMAN SOUL
> WILL NEVER BE FOUND IN ANOTHER.
>
> —Elizabeth Cady Stanton

Now What?

At this point, after increasing your awareness of your strengths and weaknesses, most self-help books would encourage you to use your newfound awareness to fix your weaknesses. That is the exact opposite of what I'm going to recommend. I don't want you to fix your weaknesses. I want you to accept them and to discover that your weaknesses are important clues to your strengths. That is the subject of the next chapter: acceptance.

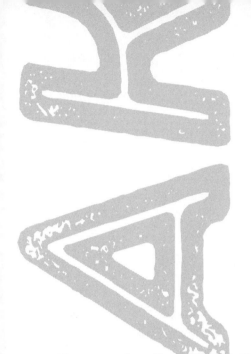

2. ACCEPTANCE

· ·

**STRONG PEOPLE ALWAYS HAVE STRONG WEAKNESSES
TOO. WHERE THERE ARE PEAKS, THERE ARE VALLEYS.**

—Peter Drucker

In the previous chapter on awareness, I offered strategies for uncovering and understanding your strengths and weaknesses. Once we are aware of our weaknesses, we need to resist the impulse to correct them. The second step in maximizing your freak factor is to accept the inevitability of weaknesses and identify the strengths that correspond with each weakness.

Reframing

Recently, my dad saw a girl wearing a T-shirt that said, "I'm not bossy. I just know what you should be doing." I found another one that says, "I'm not bossy, I just have better ideas." Both of these messages reframe bossiness, an apparent weakness, as the possession of superior knowledge, an obvious strength. Sheryl Sandberg, COO of Facebook, believes that this is an important distinction. She believes that men and boys are more likely to be praised for having the strength of leadership, while women and girls are more likely to be criticized for having the weakness of being bossy. She has made it her mission to reframe bossiness as a positive quality for women.

It may seem that reframing is just denial, dishonesty, or spin control, but it's not. Each of us has unique characteristics, and those characteristics have both positive and negative features. These features, which we usually refer to as strengths and weaknesses, cannot be separated. They come in pairs. The positive and negative elements are inextricably linked. It's common to believe that there's nothing strong about your particular weaknesses or the weaknesses of others. However, every weakness has a corresponding strength.

**THE GREAT EPOCHS OF OUR LIFE COME WHEN
WE GAIN THE COURAGE TO RECHRISTEN
OUR EVIL AS WHAT IS BEST IN US.**

—Friedrich Nietzsche, *Beyond Good and Evil*

The following is a chart of weaknesses and their corresponding strengths.

1. Make a list of the top five strengths and weaknesses that you identified in the last chapter.

2. Put a check mark next to each of them on the chart below.

3. Circle any matches. A match is when you chose both a strength and its corresponding weakness (for example, 7. Dynamic, Active and 7. Frantic, Restless).

4. For those traits that didn't match, identify the corresponding strength or weaknesses. Does that trait describe you? If so, circle that match as well.

X	Strengths	Weaknesses	X
	1. Creative, Innovative	1. Chaotic, Disorganized	
	2. Organized, Systematic	2. Rigid, Inflexible	
	3. Dedicated, Persistent	3. Stubborn, Obstinate	
	4. Flexible, Adaptable	4. Inconsistent, Unreliable	
	5. Enthusiastic, Passionate	5. Quick-Tempered, Angry	
	6. Calm, Laid-Back	6. Unfeeling, Emotionless	
	7. Dynamic, Active	7. Frantic, Restless	
	8. Reflective, Thoughtful	8. Quiet, Shy	
	9. Adventurous, Courageous	9. Reckless, Irresponsible	
	10. Responsible, Cautious	10. Boring, Uninteresting	
	11. Activist, Revolutionary	11. Rebellious, Radical	
	12. Conventional, Traditional	12. Old-Fashioned, Conforming	
	13. Direct, Honest	13. Blunt, Rude	
	14. Polite, Courteous	14. Superficial, Insincere	
	15. Cooperative, Helpful	15. Passive, Submissive	
	16. Competitive, Assertive	16. Antagonistic, Aggressive	
	17. Theoretical, Idealistic	17. Unrealistic, Impractical	
	18. Realistic, Practical	18. Negative, Critical	
	19. Independent, Self-Sufficient	19. Isolated, Selfish	
	20. Team Player, Unselfish	20. Dependent, Needy	
	21. Objective, Unbiased	21. Detached, Insensitive	
	22. Sensitive, Caring	22. Vulnerable, Emotional	
	23. Humble, Modest	23. Timid, Insecure	
	24. Confident, Secure	24. Arrogant, Conceited	
	25. Patient, Cautious	25. Slow, Indecisive	
	26. Spontaneous, Instinctive	26. Impatient, Impulsive	
	27. Influential, Powerful	27. Controlling, Manipulative	

X	Strengths	Weaknesses	X
	28. Obedient, Dutiful	28. Weak, Subservient	
	29. Motivated, Ambitious	29. Obsessive, Workaholic	
	30. Relaxed, Easygoing	30. Unmotivated, Lazy	
	31. Analytical, Rational	31. Critical, Judgmental	
	32. Compassionate, Sympathetic	32. Lenient, Indulgent	
	33. Positive, Encouraging	33. Flattering, Naive	
	34. Realistic, Sensible	34. Negative, Discouraging	
	35. Open-Minded, Tolerant	35. Unprincipled, Naive	
	36. Certain, Decisive	36. Opinionated, Dogmatic	
	37. Extravagant, Elegant	37. Complicated, Difficult	
	38. Simple, Natural	38. Plain, Dull	
	39. Self-Controlled, Disciplined	39. Harsh, Stiff	
	40. Fun, Entertaining	40. Hedonistic, Self-Indulgent	
	41. Serious, Mature	41. Humorless, Solemn	
	42. Funny, Amusing	42. Silly, Immature	
	43. Focused	43. Limited, Restricted, Narrow	
	44. Exploring, Discovering	44. Distractible, Unfocused	
	45. Generous, Altruistic	45. Pushover, Sucker	
	46. Frugal, Thrifty	46. Stingy, Cheap	
	47. Curious, Inquisitive	47. Intrusive, Nosy	
	48. Content, Satisfied	48. Apathetic, Indifferent	
	49. Loyal, Devoted	49. Robotic, Gullible	
	50. Adaptable, Flexible	50. Disloyal, Fickle	
	51. Detail-Oriented, Meticulous	51. Perfectionist, Compulsive	
	52. Global, General	52. Sloppy, Careless	

WHEN I UNDERSTAND THIS LIABILITY AS A TRADE-OFF FOR MY STRENGTHS, SOMETHING NEW AND LIBERATING ARISES WITHIN ME. I NO LONGER WANT TO HAVE MY LIABILITY "FIXED."

—Parker Palmer

The Myth of Perfection

Instead of seeing weaknesses as natural and unavoidable consequences of corresponding strengths, many people see weaknesses as problems to be eliminated. As I explained earlier, when I ask students and seminar participants if they should fix weaknesses, build strengths, or do both, most choose to do both (fix weaknesses and build strengths).

→ 52 percent agreed and only 35 percent disagreed with the statement, "If I want to improve, I need to fix my weaknesses."

→ 52 percent agreed and only 33 percent disagreed with the statement, "It is important to be well-rounded, especially at work."

→ 52 percent agreed and only 30 percent disagreed with the statement, "I should fix my weaknesses and build my strengths."

→ 56 percent agreed and only 26 percent disagreed with the statement, "A well-balanced set of characteristics will make me more marketable."

As you can see, the majority of respondents to the freak factor survey choose to fix weaknesses and become well-rounded. There are a number of problems with this approach. First, efforts to eliminate weaknesses are doomed to fail, because, as I have shown, any characteristic can be considered a strength or a weakness.

Strengths	Weaknesses
1. Creative, Innovative	1. Chaotic, Disorganized
2. Organized, Systematic	2. Rigid, Inflexible

For example, consider the first pair of strengths and weaknesses in the chart (creative and disorganized versus organized and inflexible). Creative people tend to be disorganized. Because they think "outside of the box," they tend to have difficulty putting things away in boxes. Fixing the weakness of disorganization doesn't make you better. It just makes you less creative and more organized.

Organized people tend to be inflexible, because they want everything in the right box and believe that there is a box and a color-coded label for everything. Fixing the weakness of inflexibility doesn't make you better. It just makes you less organized and more creative.

Fixing a weakness doesn't make you stronger. It just trades one weakness for another.

TO WISH YOU WERE SOMEONE ELSE IS TO WASTE THE PERSON YOU ARE.

—Friedrich Nietzsche

Strengths	Weaknesses
5. Enthusiastic, Passionate	5. Quick-Tempered, Angry
6. Calm, Laid-Back	6. Unfeeling, Emotionless

You might have noticed that the fifty-two strengths and weaknesses on the chart are divided into twenty-six pairs. Each strength in the pair is the opposite of the other. For example, (1) creative is the opposite of (2) organized, and (5) enthusiastic is the opposite of (6) calm. It isn't possible to be both more enthusiastic and calmer. Becoming more enthusiastic requires you to become less calm.

I've tried to illustrate this visually in the following diagram. As you maximize your score on enthusiasm (10), it minimizes your score on calmness (0). As you maximize your score on calmness (10), it minimizes your score on enthusiasm (0). Attempting to have a little of both just leaves you with a mediocre score on both enthusiasm (5) and calmness (5). Because they are opposites, you can't increase them both at the same time.

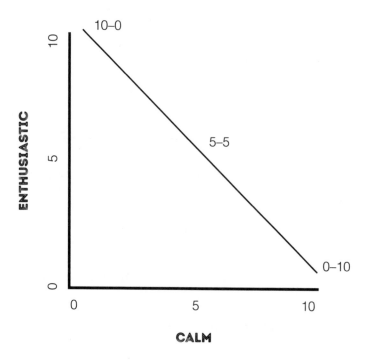

Because of this relationship between strengths and weaknesses, the best approach is to maximize whichever strength/weakness combination that you already have (since this is your natural style) at the expense of the opposing combination.

Patient, Cautious	Slow, Indecisive
Spontaneous, Instinctive	Impatient, Impulsive

GOOD THINGS MAY COME TO THOSE WHO WAIT, BUT ONLY THE THINGS LEFT BY THOSE WHO HUSTLE.

—Abraham Lincoln

This quote from Lincoln shows that although patience is a virtue, it isn't without its limitations. Patience can also be slowness and indecisiveness. Impatience, an apparent weakness, can also be beneficial when it causes us to move quickly and create new opportunities. Since every weakness has a corresponding strength, replacing a weakness with a strength just adds a different weakness.

Independent, Self-Sufficient	Isolated, Selfish
Team Player, Unselfish	Dependent, Needy

LIKE I ALWAYS SAY, THERE'S NO "I" IN "TEAM." THERE IS A "ME," THOUGH, IF YOU JUMBLE IT UP.

—David Shore

Cooperation is certainly beneficial, and many people are good team players. However, independence is also a positive characteristic, and strong individual performers don't always play well with the other boys and girls. As Michael Jordan explained, "There's no 'I' in 'team,' but there is an 'I' in 'win.'"

When you choose anything, you reject everything else ...

**SO WHEN YOU TAKE ONE COURSE OF ACTION
YOU GIVE UP ALL THE OTHER COURSES.**

—G. K. Chesterton

The second reason that fixing weaknesses doesn't work is that we have limited resources. Most people have too much to do and not enough time or energy to do it. It requires more time and energy to try to fix weakness and build strengths rather than focusing exclusively on building strengths. I'll talk about the limits of self-control later in this chapter.

Third, focusing on both strengths and weaknesses limits progress. We end up with the worst of both worlds, expending a lot of effort without achieving the desired results. This prevents us from becoming exceptional in any one area.

**LIMITATIONS AND LIABILITIES ARE
THE FLIP SIDE OF OUR GIFTS...
A PARTICULAR WEAKNESS IS THE INEVITABLE
TRADE-OFF FOR A PARTICULAR STRENGTH.**

—Parker Palmer, *Let Your Life Speak*

The same principle applies to individuals. While you are busy diffusing your time and energy broadly, in an effort to improve in a variety of different areas, other people are obsessively developing their strengths and flaunting their weaknesses. They aren't allowing their weaknesses to distract them from focusing on the areas in which they have the greatest potential. If you want to win in your career or your business, you need to be single-minded. Don't let your weaknesses and the goal of being well-rounded keep you from a maniacal focus on improving your strengths.

Finally, and most important, since weaknesses and strengths are linked, attempting to fix a weakness can actually diminish the corresponding strength.

> **IF YOU THINK A WEAKNESS CAN BE TURNED INTO A STRENGTH, I HATE TO TELL YOU THIS, BUT THAT'S ANOTHER WEAKNESS.**
>
> —Jack Handey, *Deep Thoughts*

FAMOUS FREAK: John Grisham

John Grisham is one of the most successful authors of the last twenty years. Starting with *A Time to Kill*, his legal thrillers have been read by millions and seen by millions more after being made into feature films. If effectiveness requires us to be well-rounded and balanced, then you'd expect to find those characteristics in the lives of exceptional people, such as Grisham. But you don't.

Grisham has obvious weaknesses, but he's not trying to fix them. He accepts them and refuses to change. In the Author's Note section of Grisham's recent book, *The Confession*, he writes: "Some overly observant readers may stumble across a fact or two that might appear to be in error. They may consider writing letters to point out my shortcomings. They should conserve paper. There are mistakes in this book, as always, and as long as I continue to loathe research, while at the same time remaining perfectly content to occasionally dress up the facts, I'm afraid the mistakes will continue. My hope is that the errors are insignificant in nature."

What can we learn from Grisham's example?

→ Grisham isn't listening to the criticism ("conserve paper").

→ He admits the flaws ("there are mistakes").

→ He explains that he is the source of the flaws ("loathe research ... content to occasionally dress up the facts").

→ He refuses to change, to fix the flaws ("mistakes will continue").

→ He reminds us that the flaws don't matter that much ("the errors are insignificant").

Even if it is possible to repair or even eliminate our weaknesses, what will it cost? What talents are we destroying in the process of fixing our apparent shortcomings? Make sure you are ready to pay the price before you start renovating your life.

WE ARE SO ACCUSTOMED TO DISGUISE OURSELVES TO OTHERS THAT, IN THE END, WE BECOME DISGUISED TO OURSELVES.

—Francois de La Rochefoucauld

The Myth of Unlimited Potential

"But can't we change?" This is a common question that I hear after sharing *The Freak Factor* with people. My answer is that people don't change that much. For example, in college, I studied psychology and later earned a graduate degree in counseling psychology. Unfortunately, during my course work, I discovered that counseling required two skills that I didn't have: sitting still and listening. So much for that. It is important to note that during my time in school, I received extensive training in empathy, listening, collaboration, group process, nonverbal communication, personality, and behavior change. Despite this knowledge, I couldn't seem to change my behavior or transform my personality. I wasn't any better at sitting still, listening, or doing what I was told. I tried to change. I wanted to change. I put years of effort into changing, but it didn't work.

EVERY LIMIT IS A BEGINNING AS WELL AS AN ENDING.

— George Eliot

An article in the *New York Times* entitled "Can You Become a Creature of New Habits?" explains the science behind our inability to change. We are born with the ability to deal with challenges in a variety of ways, but during puberty "the brain shuts down half of that capacity, preserving only those modes of thought that have seemed most valuable during the first decade or so of life … This breaks the major rule in the American belief system—that anyone can do anything. That's a lie that we have perpetuated, and it fosters mediocrity. Knowing what you're good at and doing even more of it creates excellence."[1]

We can change. We can improve. We can grow. However, our growth and development efforts should build on existing strengths, not attempt to overcome weaknesses. Apparently, the brain is designed to build on past patterns of success, not to create completely new ones.

YOU CAN'T PUT FEATHERS ON A DOG AND CALL IT A CHICKEN.

— Dr. Phil McGraw

We can't change our fundamental natures. Attempts to do so are slow, painful, frustrating, and ultimately ineffective. Even if modest improvements are made, there isn't much of a payoff. Unfortunately, we've been taught that we can be whatever we want to be and that, with enough self-control, we can do anything.

The Myth of Self-Control

What do you want? Do you want to be more organized, lose weight, get a promotion, or have a better marriage? Most self-help books have one primary suggestion on how to do this: use self-discipline to simply act differently. They argue that if we just wanted it bad enough, we'd be able to make the change. In this view, people succeed because they have self-control and fail because they lack self-control. I disagree.

1 | Janet Rae-Dupree, "Can You Become a Creature of New Habits?" New York Times, May 4, 2008, http://www.nytimes.com/2008/05/04/business/04unbox.html?_r=1&.

There are three parts to the myth of self-control. First, we believe that people have unlimited potential. We are taught that we can do anything if we are just willing to try hard enough. Therefore, if we aren't successful, it is not because of a lack of ability; it is because of a lack of effort. The second belief is directly tied to the first. We believe that self-discipline is the route to success. If we just had more self-control, we could achieve our goals. Third, we believe that success is the result of perseverance. If we just tried hard enough and long enough, if we could stick with it over time and never give up, then we could succeed.

The truth is that everyone has the same amount of self-control. The key to success is determining how you will use the self-control that you have. In other words, you don't need more fuel; you just need to become more fuel-efficient. I believe that we all have the same amount of self-control. You don't get more or less than anyone else. Successful people do not have extra discipline; they just use what they have more wisely.

DISCIPLINE AND CONCENTRATION ARE A MATTER OF BEING INTERESTED.

—Tom Kite

The June 2007 edition of *Men's Health* magazine explains that "dieting can increase the likelihood that you'll spend your money impulsively. Why? The scientists theorize that you have only a limited number of mental resources to allocate toward self-control. If you're using these resources to resist certain food cravings, you become more prone to giving in to other temptations."

As Roy Baumeister at Florida State University explains, "Self-control comes in limited quantities and must be replenished." Self-control is more like a renewable energy source than a learned skill. After individuals completed tasks requiring self-control, they had "less physical stamina and impulse control." Baumeister's experiments showed that "resisting temptation consumed an important resource (self-control), which was then less available to help the person persist in the face of failure."

Similarly, in her book *The Happiness Project*, Gretchen Rubin discovered that "relying on willpower is very hard—so whenever possible, I abandon it. ... Because self-control is a precious resource, try to use it as little as possible. Look for ways to engineer situations so they don't test your willpower at all."

> **IT'S VERY DIFFICULT TO MOTIVATE**
> **YOURSELF TO DO SOMETHING.**
> **IT'S MUCH EASIER TO LEVERAGE WHAT YOU**
> **ARE ALREADY MOTIVATED TO DO.**
>
> —Chris Guillebeau, *The Art of Non-Conformity*

We often have difficulty when we are using our discipline in the wrong places, like trying to fix our weaknesses and trying to fit in by being someone we're not. These activities drain our energy and sap our self-discipline.

> **PEOPLE THINK I'M DISCIPLINED.**
> **IT'S NOT DISCIPLINE, IT IS DEVOTION.**
> **THERE IS A GREAT DIFFERENCE.**
>
> —Luciano Pavarotti

How can we use our energy more efficiently? How can we get more out of our limited supply of self-control? We need to build on strengths instead of trying to fix weaknesses. We need to develop our positive characteristics instead of trying to change our natural preferences. These activities are fueled by devotion, not discipline. They rely on passion instead of pain.

Devotion is a great substitute for discipline. Discipline is scarce, but devotion is abundant. Discipline is painful, but devotion is enjoyable. Both discipline and devotion act as fuel for our activities, and we can choose which one we will use. It takes tremendous discipline to fix our weaknesses, but devotion provides the energy for building on our strengths.

We've seen that each of our weaknesses has a corresponding strength. Because of this, we need to reframe our unique characteristics in a positive, instead of negative, way. We need to wave our freak flags high. We'll explore this more in the next chapter: appreciation.

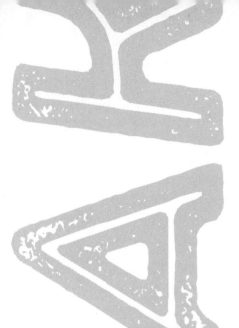

3. APPRECIATION

WHITE COLLAR CONSERVATIVE FLASHIN' DOWN THE
STREET, POINTING THAT PLASTIC FINGER AT ME.
THEY ALL ASSUME MY KIND WILL DROP AND DIE,
BUT I'M GONNA WAVE MY FREAK FLAG HIGH.

— Jimi Hendrix

The following stories show how seemingly obvious weaknesses actually conceal surprising strengths. These examples illustrate the unique relationship between strengths and weaknesses. It is my hope that these examples will move you from simply accepting your weaknesses to having an intense appreciation for your apparent flaws.

OUR STRENGTH GROWS OUT OF OUR WEAKNESS.

—Ralph Waldo Emerson, "Compensation"

Disorganization

It's good to be neat, and it's bad to be messy—at least, that's what we're told. We've all heard that "cleanliness is next to godliness" and "a cluttered desk is a sign of a cluttered mind." Furthermore, most people believe that they would be happier and more successful if they were more organized. This desire is evidenced by the success of the Container Store and the endless list of television shows dedicated to cleaning up and reorganizing messy homes. Being disorganized seems like an obvious weakness that needs to be fixed, right?

Not necessarily. In *A Perfect Mess: The Hidden Benefits of Disorder*, David Freedman and Eric Abrahamson argue that messiness is actually a strength and should be "celebrated rather than avoided." They provide evidence that there are significant benefits to disorder. Andy Rooney, the quirky commentator for *60 Minutes*, agreed, saying, "Creativity doesn't come out of order; it comes out of messiness."

For example, Alexander Fleming discovered penicillin while sorting through his cluttered lab after returning from a long vacation. If his lab had been clean and organized, we might not have access to life-saving antibiotics. Albert Einstein, probably one of the most creative minds of the twentieth century, challenged the enemies of clutter by asking, "If a cluttered desk is a sign of a cluttered mind, then what is an empty desk a sign of?"

ROUGH DIAMONDS MAY SOMETIMES BE MISTAKEN FOR WORTHLESS PEBBLES.

— Sir Thomas Browne

Dyslexia

Dyslexia is a disability. People with dyslexia get letters and words mixed up, and this leads to major problems with reading and writing. This, in turn, is a major barrier to success—or is it?

Don Wells, a wonderful friend and consultant, sent me this story about Tommy:

> When I was head of the middle school at the Friends School, there was a 14-year-old, Tommy, who was severely dyslexic. I ran a six week course about perception with about 15 students in it. One day I said that we were going for a stroll about the school grounds and when we returned I would ask them 20 questions about things that we would see on our walk. For example, were there any red cars in the parking lot? They could take any notes that

they wanted to, and the things that I would ask would not be trick questions.

We walked and everyone took notes and looked earnestly, except Tommy. He just strolled along and observed. That was it. When we got back to the classroom, I gave everyone a piece of paper with 20 questions on it. There were some very smart kids in the classroom, and it was well known that Tommy struggled in almost every class.

Kids finished and exchanged papers and then we went down the answers. The highest score out of 20 seemed to be 14, by perhaps the smartest kid in the class. However, Tommy got 18 out of 20! The class and I were stunned. They asked "how do you do it?" Tommy, a bit embarrassed, simply said "I just looked."

Students were not convinced, so they persuaded me, and Tommy, to do it again in the next class. We did and got the same results as he blew everyone else away, even though kids were watching him for any clues.

His mom and Tommy struggled greatly about the stigma of his performance in school. But from that day on Tommy was never dismissed as dumb. He simply viewed things with a different eye than others and it worked. His mom, a few days afterward, came into my office and hugged me while sobbing saying that Tommy's life changed that day. What a gift! Tommy went on to graduate from North Carolina State with a degree in design and has a successful business near Memphis.

Tommy isn't alone. A recent study by Julie Logan, professor of entrepreneurship at the Cass Business School in London, showed that 35 percent of small business owners have dyslexia. This is significant because only 10 percent of Americans have dyslexia. Another study in the United Kingdom found that people with dyslexia are far more likely to become millionaires. In fact, almost half of the millionaires in the sample had dyslexia.

A well-known person who appreciates his weaknesses is Sir Richard Branson, billionaire and founder of the Virgin Group. When asked if his dyslexia has hindered his business success, Branson said, "Strangely, I think my dyslexia has helped." Other famous individuals who've lived with learning disabilities include John Chambers, CEO of Cisco Systems; Ingvar Kamprad, founder of IKEA; and Charles Schwab, founder of the discount brokerage firm that bears his name.

What explains this apparent relationship between disability and success? Researchers believe that "most people who make a million [dollars] have difficult childhoods or have been frustrated in a major way. Dyslexia is one of the driving forces behind that." Having dyslexia makes the person a freak and leaves him or her "outside of the mainstream social groups in school."

However, it seems that dyslexia is a double-edged sword. The obvious weaknesses and problems of dyslexia are accompanied by important strengths. Logan's research concluded that "dyslexics were more likely than non-dyslexics to delegate authority and to excel in oral communication and problem solving and were twice as likely to own two or more businesses." Experts suggest that people with dyslexia are often better than most at being "creative and looking at the bigger picture," and this can make them better strategic thinkers. Additionally, "individuals who have difficulty reading and writing tend to deploy other strengths." They focus on their unique abilities instead of their disability.

Addiction

Todd Crandell had been a drug addict for almost fifteen years. He was homeless, destitute, afraid, and alone. He had lost everything that mattered to him. But in 2007, he founded a successful nonprofit organization and became the author of the best-selling *Racing for Recovery: From Addict to Ironman*. He has completed numerous Ironman Triathlons (consisting of a 2.4-mile swim, a 112-mile bike ride, and a 26.2-mile run) and has a loving wife and four children.

How did Crandell transform his life? He harnessed his addiction. He hasn't really stopped being an addict. He's just addicted to something new: Ironman Triathlons.

Crandell's former coach put it this way: "He's changed his addiction to a positive addiction and he's now used it as a platform to help others. And so, he has no choice, his body's going to have to fall apart before he'll stop."

Crandell is still abusing his body. He's still obsessed. He's still addicted. ESPN reporter Tom Rinaldi put it this way: "He found his new focus in a passion as extreme as his addiction, the grueling pursuit of a triathlon."

WHAT IF THERE WERE ADDICTIONS THAT, INSTEAD OF MAKING YOU WEAKER, MADE YOU STRONGER?

—William Glasser, psychiatrist and
author of *Positive Addiction*

Crandell's weakness was his intensity, but it was also his strength. In an interview, he said, "The same tenacity I put into destroying myself, I just needed to switch it and put it into repairing myself." Crandell isn't a new person. He hasn't undergone a fundamental change in personality. He has just discovered and applied the positive aspects of his unique personality.

So it isn't surprising that Crandell didn't stop with just one new addiction. He also founded Racing for Recovery, a nonprofit organization that helps addicts find hope and health through athletic pursuits. However, "providing that hope became Crandell's new addiction, but like his old one, it's come with great financial and emotional cost."

Crandell lost everything again. He had cars repossessed and houses foreclosed, and that was after becoming sober. His financial losses were due to his fanatical pursuit of the organization's mission, and he made no apologies. "How can you look at who I was and who I am today and not say 'this is what I'm supposed to do?'" Crandell can't do anything just a little. He can't take it easy. He can't slow down. His strength is his weakness. The two are inseparable. His pursuit of the Ironman is "an addiction, perhaps, but also a mission and a purpose—to keep making the journey from addict to inspiration."

Insanity

The ancient philosopher Seneca said that "there is no great genius without a touch of madness." In his mind, genius and insanity aren't two separate conditions; they are both part of the same condition. If you have one, you have the other.

Apple celebrates the connection between genius and madness in its "Think different" commercial: "Here's to the crazy ones, the misfits, the rebels, the troublemakers, the round pegs in the square holes, the ones who see things differently. They're not fond of rules and they have no respect for the status quo. You can quote them, disagree with them, glorify or vilify them. About the only thing you can't do is ignore them. Because they change things. They push the human race forward. And while some may see them as the crazy ones, we see genius. Because the people who are crazy enough to think they can change the world are the ones who do. Think Different."

Unfortunately, not everyone appreciates people who are different. A few months after my friend's son, Jim, started kindergarten, the teacher diagnosed him as having attention deficit hyperactivity disorder and oppositional defiant disorder, which is defined as a pattern of angry, hostile, and disobedient behavior. Naturally, my friends were concerned about their son and had him evaluated by a psychologist. The tests showed that he had an IQ in the genius range. He didn't have a problem. He had a gift that looked like a problem.

I think this happens more than we think. Every day, bosses, teachers, spouses, coworkers, and friends misdiagnose genius as madness. Sometimes we even do it to ourselves. Once this happens, the attempts at healing begin. Unfortunately, healing the madness can destroy the genius.

Kay Redfield Jamison, PhD, a professor of psychiatry at the Johns Hopkins University School of Medicine, also supports Seneca's argument. Jamison wrote a fascinating book, *Touched with Fire: Manic-Depressive Illness and the Artistic Temperament,* which suggests that mental illness might actually be a requirement for creating great art.

Jamison argues that "most artistic geniuses were (and are) manic depressives" and that "psychological suffering is an essential component of artistic creativity." This might seem like a wild proposition. So it is also important to note that Kay is a scientist and has researched this connection extensively. She also has manic depression, or bipolar disorder.

The most astonishing response to Jamison's book comes from Robert Bernard Martin, professor emeritus at Princeton University: "By the end of the book the reader has been quietly rerouted to the profoundly ethical question of whether the eradication of this disease (manic-depression) by modern molecular biology would not ultimately be a diminution of the human race."

That is a strong statement. Martin is implying that curing bipolar disorder could diminish people's ability to create fine art. If this is true, then fostering this condition might increase people's creative impulses.

Michael Maccoby, author of *The Productive Narcissist,* believes that the negative characteristics of narcissistic leaders (extreme sensitivity to criticism, unwillingness to listen, paranoia, extreme competitiveness, anger, exaggeration, isolation, and grandiosity) are inextricably tied to their positive characteristics (independent thinking, passion, charisma, voracious learning, perseverance, sense of humor, risk taking, and desire to change the world). His research shows that it isn't possible to benefit from the advantages of the narcissistic personality without suffering from the disadvantages. They are inextricably linked.

Similarly, in *A First-Rate Madness*, Nassir Ghaemi argues that leaders with mental illnesses are more effective than those who are mentally healthy. In *America's Obsessives*, Joshua Kendall shares the stories of Thomas Jefferson, Henry Heinz, Estée Lauder, and others to demonstrate the relationship between obsessive compulsive disorder and extraordinary success. Finally, Kevin Dutton wrote *The Wisdom of Psychopaths* to expose the surprising strengths and positive characteristics of people who are psychopaths.

**I USED TO SEE TOURETTE'S AS A CURSE,
BUT NOW I CONSIDER IT A BLESSING.
IT'S MADE ME WHO I AM.**

—Dave Pittman, *American Idol* contestant

Conviction

Catherine Rohr is the founder of Defy Ventures, an organization that provides inmates with the equivalent of an MBA degree. Rohr believes that prisoners can succeed after their release if they have the right tools, and Defy Ventures provides them with the support and education that they need to build legitimate businesses.

Rohr is a former Wall Street investor who toured a prison and "noticed that executives and inmates had more in common than most would think. They know how to manage others to get things done. Even the most unsophisticated drug dealers inherently understand business concepts such as competition, profitability, risk management and proprietary sales channels. For both executives and inmates, passion is instinctive."

After having this realization, Rohr made it her goal to help inmates to develop and operate legitimate businesses. She believed that it was possible to channel the "entrepreneurial passions and influential personalities of the inmates—intentionally recruiting former gang leaders, drug dealers and hustlers." Catherine described the inmates in this way: "These men are already proven entrepreneurs." She then explained that many of Defy Venture's graduates go on to earn legitimate six-figure incomes.

Rohr's program is a phenomenal example of the power of finding strength inside apparent weakness and framing seemingly negative characteristics in a positive way. If Rohr can do this with convicted felons, what could we accomplish with our less severe flaws?

Instead of trying to be perfect, we need to appreciate our limitations and make sure that we don't let what we cannot do interfere with what we can do. Then we need to go even further. Once we've developed an appreciation for our weaknesses, we should amplify them.

PART TWO:
ACT

DIFFERENTLY

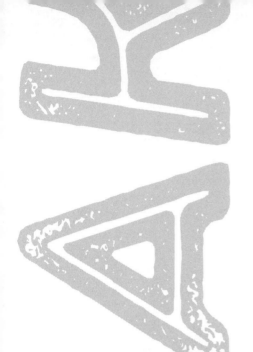

4. AMPLIFICATION

**IF EVERYTHING SEEMS UNDER CONTROL,
YOU'RE NOT GOING FAST ENOUGH.**

—Mario Andretti

Many weaknesses are framed in terms of excess. We are told that we are too organized or too messy, too quiet or too loud, too critical or too kind. I believe that these criticisms are usually incorrect. In fact, it is more likely that we don't have enough of that characteristic.

WE ARE SO ACCUSTOMED TO DISGUISE OURSELVES TO OTHERS, THAT, IN THE END WE BECOME DISGUISED TO OURSELVES.

— Francois de La Rochefoucauld

It can be difficult to amplify our weaknesses, because we are often worried that we'll be rejected for being different. As such, we often try to moderate and control our weaknesses. Unfortunately, this inhibits our distinctiveness and hampers our success. It also prevents us from achieving our potential and becoming our truest selves. The danger in trying to be what everyone else wants us to be is that we can forget who we are in the process.

Amplification is the essence of flaunting your weaknesses. According to the Encarta Dictionary, *flaunt* means "to parade yourself without shame. Show something off—to display something ostentatiously." This is a great description. Too often, we are uncomfortable with our weaknesses. We are ashamed of them, apologize for them, and try to hide them. My goal in this book isn't simply to help you become comfortable with your weaknesses. I want you to parade them without shame. I want you to show them off.

For example, Jimmy Vee at Gravitational Marketing calls himself "The Five-Foot High Marketing Guy." He doesn't try to hide or minimize his short stature. He celebrates it, which makes him likable, memorable, and interesting.

YOU CAN ONLY BE YOUNG ONCE. BUT YOU CAN ALWAYS BE IMMATURE.

—Dave Barry

Jimmy Kimmel is a comedian and the host of the late-night talk show *Jimmy Kimmel Live!* Because of his success, he was asked to host the White House Correspondents' Dinner. At one point during the event, Kimmel walked up to the podium and said, "I also want to thank Mr. Mills, my high school history teacher, who told me that I'd never amount to anything if I didn't stop screwing around in class. Mr. Mills, I'm about to high-five the president of the United States of America." Then he stepped over and high-fived Barack Obama. When Kimmel came back to the podium, he said, "Eat it, Mills."

I'm not going to criticize Mr. Mills. He believed, as many people do, that school success is essential for success in life. He was trying to give Kimmel helpful advice.

But let's look at how Kimmel actually succeeded: He didn't stop screwing around. He went pro. He got sillier, more ridiculous, more childish, and more immature. He started screwing around for a living. He went further in the direction that Mr. Mills told him not to go. Kimmel amplified his weakness, and that is when he found success.

Most people would agree with the ideas in this book, as long as you don't take them too far. It is fine to build on your strengths, within reason. It is good to embrace your weaknesses, within reason. Go ahead and pursue your passion, within reason. Be yourself, within reason. But that is the problem. My point is that you need to go even further in the direction that everyone is telling you not to go.

WE ARE ALL AGREED THAT YOUR THEORY IS CRAZY. THE QUESTION WHICH DIVIDES US IS WHETHER IT IS CRAZY ENOUGH TO HAVE A CHANCE OF BEING CORRECT. MY OWN FEELING IS THAT IT IS NOT CRAZY ENOUGH.

—Niels Bohr, to Wolfgang Pauli

Are you a bad singer? Maybe you're not bad enough. William Hung achieved fame as a contestant on *American Idol,* a reality show for aspiring singers. His singing was so bad that he caught the attention of the judges and of the rest of America. Hung subsequently appeared on *The Tonight Show* with Jay Leno and *Today.* Hung went on to record an album that sold almost two hundred thousand copies.

Are you too cynical? Maybe you are not cynical enough. The people at Despair.com have turned cynicism into a business by creating demotivational posters, which parody the inspirational messages that decorate corporate conference rooms across the country.

Do you eat too much? Maybe you don't eat enough. Do you eat too fast? Maybe you don't eat fast enough. Takeru Kobayashi has made a living out of speed eating. He has set world records for eating hot dogs, hamburgers, bratwurst, lobster, and dumplings.

Kobayashi has turned gluttony into a career as a member of Major League Eating. I'm not making that up—there really is a professional association for speed-eaters.

WHEN THE GOING GETS WEIRD, THE WEIRD TURN PRO.

—Hunter S. Thompson

Do you drink too much? Maybe you don't drink enough. Do you have a drinking problem? Zane Lamprey's television show, *Three Sheets*, follows him "around the world, one drink at a time." He's getting paid to get drunk. Maybe you can turn your problem into a career, fame, or both.

Are you too neurotic? Maybe you aren't neurotic enough. When Chris Martin of the band Coldplay was interviewed on *60 Minutes*, the interviewer explained that Martin has a habit of making rules and writing notes and lists on everything, including his body and furniture. He concluded his description of Martin by saying, "Like many artists he is openly, gloriously neurotic." Shortly after the interview, Coldplay won Grammy Awards for song of the year and rock album of the year.

It is tempting to believe that Martin and his band are successful despite his neuroticism. However, I think he is successful because he embraces and flaunts his neurotic impulses. I think we need to follow his example and be "openly, gloriously" weak. Just replace "neurotic" with your particular weakness, and then ask yourself what you would do differently if you were going to do it openly and gloriously.

For example, I'm openly and gloriously hyperactive. After I ran my first forty-mile ultramarathon, my brother-in-law told me that I was crazy and awesome. One of the main lessons of this book is that being crazy might be an important part of being awesome. But there is another important lesson in this example: Millions of children, mostly boys, spend their childhoods being criticized for being hyperactive. I was no exception. I wished I could sit still, but I couldn't. I loved recess. I loved gym. I loved athletic practices and games. But my love of activity was considered a weakness.

Now, as an adult, I run marathons and ultramarathons and compete in triathlons. When most people hear about my accomplishments, they say, "Wow! I could never do that." Instead of seeing my hyperactivity as a problem, they see it as a strength they wish that they had. This is an important turning point. You will know that you have gone far enough—that you are amplifying your weaknesses—when people start to praise you for the very things that they used to criticize you for.

PUT ALL YOUR EGGS IN ONE BASKET, AND WATCH THAT BASKET!

— Mark Twain

Obsession has a bad reputation. We use it most often in a negative way. The most notable example is the psychological diagnosis of obsessive compulsive disorder (OCD). However, just as with the term *freak*, I think obsession can be a very positive thing. Successful people are obsessed with what they do. In fact, obsession might be an absolute necessity for world-class performance.

In his book *Talent is Overrated*, Geoff Colvin explains that the superstars in every field, from sports to music to art, have one thing in common. It took at least ten years, or ten thousand hours, of intense and deliberate practice for those superstars to become the best. In other words, they had to demonstrate an obsessive discipline in order to rise to the top. They had to become addicts.

I saw this obsession demonstrated vividly in the documentary *Comedian*, which features Jerry Seinfeld and Orny Adams. The film follows Seinfeld as he began to rebuild his stand-up comedy routine with all-new material after the phenomenal success of his TV show. Before touring with his new routine, Seinfeld spent more than six months perfecting each line, performing late at night in basement comedy clubs throughout New York City.

The movie opens with a quote from a comedy club owner: "There is a certain compulsion among stand-up comedians to go on stage and perform." But don't mistake that compulsion for weakness. Comedians' compulsion is an absolute necessity if they want to continue to be the funniest comedians in the world. Their compulsion—their addiction—is what drives them to obsessively and endlessly practice their craft, and it is that constant practice that makes them the best.

Addiction = Obsessive Practice = Greatness

Greatness starts with addiction. Without the addiction, without the obsession, without the compulsion, and without the inescapable need, there is no practice, and thus there is no greatness.

What are you addicted to? What do you need? What can't you live without? What do you do too much, too often, and for too long?

How can you build on your addiction and become the best? How can you use the power of your addiction to fuel the obsessive practice that it takes to become one of the best in the world?

Outrageous Rewards

Sometimes we seem to confuse being "not bad" with being "good," but they're not the same thing. There are huge rewards for being good, and even more so for being the best. Meanwhile, there is virtually no payoff for being mediocre or average.

What is it worth to be the best? Why bother trying to become the best? What's so bad about being average?

To answer those questions, let's consider book sales. If you write an average book, it will sell five hundred copies. That is probably not even enough to cover the publishing and marketing costs. The vast majority of books—90 percent—don't even do that well, selling less than one hundred copies. As this example illustrates, it doesn't pay to be mediocre.

But what about best sellers? The best books can sell more than a million copies. Authors of these books make enough from sales to retire early and live on their own private island in the Caribbean. It is like winning the lottery. Do you want to be average, or do you want to be the best?

THE FREAK FACTOR

The value of being the best can be seen more clearly by looking at book sales on Amazon.com. The following are the average daily book sales based on sales rank:

Sales Rank	Number Sold	Revenue ($)
1	2,100	4,200
10	220	440
100	50	100
1,000	11	22
10,000	2	4
100,000	1	2

The #1 book on Amazon.com sells more books in one day than the #100,000 book will sell in six years and more books in two days than the #10,000 book sells in an entire year! Even estimating a small royalty of $2 per book, the #1 book earns $4,200 per day for the author, while the #100,000 book earns just $730 per year for its author. There are exceptional rewards for being exceptional. These rewards increase drastically as you move closer to the top.

The same is true in the speaking business. Statistics from the National Speakers Association show that the top 3 percent of speakers earn more than $10,000 per presentation, and the top 40 percent earn more than $5,000 per speech. These speakers earn more for one day's work than the average American earns in two months. Meanwhile, average speakers are paid in pens, plaques, gift certificates, mugs, and honorariums that barely cover their travel costs.[1]

1 | *Careers in Focus: Coaches & Fitness Professionals, Second Edition.* (New York: Ferguson, 2008), Google Books, p. 78.

Professional athletes provide even more astonishing examples. An all-conference high school baseball player will probably get a scholarship to college, avoiding school loans and other costs that most students face. If that same player can become an all-conference or All-American athlete in college, he will probably be drafted by a professional team.

Once drafted, that player will start in the minor leagues, where salaries are low and crowds are sparse. Notice that the rewards for being very good are sometimes very small. But if a player does well in the minor leagues, he might get a chance to play in the big show, Major League Baseball. The minimum salary for an MLB player was over $500,000 in 2015.[2] That is more than ten times what the average American earns in a year. The average salary for players was almost $4 million,[3] more than one hundred times the salary of the average American. The rewards are even more outrageous if you are the best of the best.

The highest-paid baseball player in 2015 will earn $30 million.[4] It would take the average American more than a thousand years to earn this amount. Even when compared with other professional baseball players, this salary is still enormous. A player who earned the league minimum, $500,000 per year, would need to play for sixty years in order to catch up with that yearly paycheck. The average

2 | Eric Stephen, "MLB Minimum Salary Set to Increase to $507,500 in 2015," www.truebluela.com, November 20, 2014, http://www.truebluela.com/2014/11/20/7178067/mlb-minimum-salary-2015

3 | Ted Berg, "The Average MLB Salary Is Over $4 Million and Players Still Get $100 A Day in Meal Money," USA Today, April 1, 2015, http://ftw.usatoday.com/2015/04/major-league-baseball-average-salary-meal-money-2015-mlb

4 | Eric Schaal, "MLB: The 8 Highest-Paid Players of 2015 (No-Yankee Edition)," Sports CheatSheet, August 7, 2015, http://www.cheatsheet.com/sports/8-highest-paid-mlb-players-of-2015-the-no-yankee-edition.html/

player would need nine years to match the same total, which is problematic, since the average career lasts less than three years.

IT IS FAR MORE LUCRATIVE TO LEVERAGE YOUR STRENGTHS, INSTEAD OF ATTEMPTING TO FIX ALL THE CHINKS IN YOUR ARMOR.

—Tim Ferriss, *The 4-Hour Work Week*

The following chart illustrates three important points. First, rewards increase exponentially as you go from being very good to being the best. Second, there are virtually no rewards for moving from below average to average. Third, your best chance at being the best is to build on your existing strengths (where you are already above average) instead of trying to remediate weaknesses (where you are below average).

Be Strong

There are three myths that keep us from building on our existing strengths. First, we believe strengths will always be there, so we don't need to worry about them. The truth, however, is that if you don't use it, you lose it. Second, we think that because we're already strong in these areas, there's not much room to improve. The truth is that our strengths are where we have the most potential.

More than thirty years ago, the board of education in Omaha, Nebraska, tested the reading comprehension of high school freshmen. They discovered that some students could only read 90 words per minute with good comprehension, while others could read 350 words per minute with the same level of comprehension. They put all the students in an Evelyn Wood speed-reading course to improve their skills. At the end of six weeks, the students who were weak readers and had only been able to read 90 words per minute had improved to 150 words per minute.

However, the students who were already strong readers improved their scores dramatically, going from 350 words per minute to almost 3,000 words per minute. We often think that we should work on our weaknesses because we have more room to improve in those areas, but this example shows that our greatest opportunities for improvement lie in our existing strengths.

The third myth that keeps us from building on our strengths is the belief that focusing on strengths will make a person one-dimensional. Mark Twain once said, "To a man with a hammer, everything looks like a nail." His point was that we sometimes use the skills that we have in situations where they aren't relevant or appropriate. Twain has a lot of great quotes, but I'd like to modify this one slightly.

"If you are a person with a hammer, start looking for nails." This is the essence of amplification. Use what you have. Don't worry about the strengths that you don't have. Seek out more situations that require what you possess. Find more things that need hammering. Find people with a broken hammer or no hammer; they need someone just like you. As Seth Godin suggests, if "a hammer is exactly the tool that will solve your problem ... Hire a guy who only uses a hammer. Odds are, he's pretty good at it ... Go to someone who has only one tool, but uses it beautifully."

There is another reason that we don't need to be worried about becoming one-dimensional: we have more than one strength. The ultimate success strategy is to combine your strengths together into a superpower to become a superfreak. For example, my top five strengths, as identified by Gallup's StrengthsFinder, are the following:

- → Input—I love to learn and read.

- → Ideation—I love ideas.

- → Command—I love to be in charge.

- → Activator—I love to get things moving.

- → Achiever—I love to get things done.

I combine all these strengths into a superpower in my work as a professional speaker. Speaking gives me the opportunity to share the ideas (Ideation) that I've learned by reading and listening to audiobooks (Input). Being the one at the front of the room with a microphone in my hand makes me the center of attention. Everyone is listening to me (Command). The fact that I'm self-employed also fulfills my need to be in charge. Additionally, I don't need external motivation to keep my speaking business going, because I'm so motivated to work on projects (Activator) and to complete those projects (Achiever). I'm a superfreak.

Furthermore, we need to remember that our strengths are patterns of passion and proficiency. They are what we love to do. They are what we do well. They are also broad abilities, not narrow skills. I can apply my Command strength in all sorts of ways and in many different situations. There are a lot of ways to take control.

I can focus my Input strength on a variety of topics. My Ideation strength allows me to see the connections between seemingly different concepts. Building our strengths doesn't make us one-dimensional, because our strengths have many dimensions.

There are three primary reasons to build your existing strengths. First, it feels good. Working on our strengths is enjoyable and energizing. Second, as we just learned, the rewards for improving our strengths are outrageous.

> **YOUR STRENGTHS HAVE THE CAPACITY TO BECOME SO DOMINANT THAT THEY RENDER YOUR LIMITATIONS IRRELEVANT.**
>
> —Dr. Lance Watson

Third, our strengths make up for our weaknesses. A well-developed strength often makes our weaknesses irrelevant. As Keith Ferrazzi explains in Never Eat Alone, "In developing an expertise that highlighted my strengths, I was able to overcome my weaknesses. The trick is not to work obsessively on the skills and talents you lack but to focus and cultivate your strengths so that your weaknesses matter less."

SUCCESS IS ACHIEVED BY DEVELOPING OUR STRENGTHS, NOT ELIMINATING OUR WEAKNESSES.

—Marilyn vos Savant

If we are going to amplify our weaknesses, then we also need to move into situations that maximize our strengths and make our weaknesses irrelevant. We need to find or create alignment between who we are, where we are, and what we do.

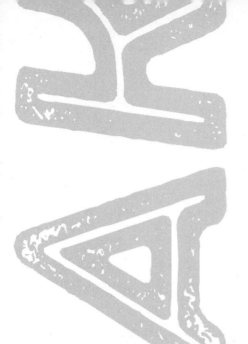

5. ALIGNMENT

• •

**EVERY INDIVIDUAL HAS A PLACE TO FILL IN THE
WORLD AND IS IMPORTANT IN SOME RESPECT,
WHETHER HE CHOOSES TO BE SO OR NOT.**

—Nathaniel Hawthorne

Too often, we try to change ourselves to fit the situation. We try to become what the boss or teacher or coach or girl or guy wants us to be. Instead, we need to find or create situations and environments that reward us for our natural style and abilities rather than punishing us for them.

The Elephant Man

Joseph Merrick lived in England during the late eighteen hundreds and was widely known as the Elephant Man. Due to his severe deformities, he was considered unemployable and spent much of his life as an attraction in a freak show. After the English government banned freak shows, Merrick was befriended by Frederick Treves, a physician at London Hospital. Merrick was treated with kindness by the hospital staff and many visitors, and he lived in the hospital until his death.

However, because of his grotesque appearance, Merrick did not anticipate that anyone would ever accept him. When he first arrived at the hospital, he asked Treves to help him find shelter at an asylum for the blind. Merrick believed, quite correctly, that his major weakness, physical abnormality, would not be a problem if he could live among people who couldn't see. He knew that how he looked would be irrelevant to the blind residents of the asylum. Furthermore, with the visual barrier removed, those residents would be able to truly "see" him and accept him for his many positive qualities.

**HIDE NOT YOUR STRENGTHS.
THEY WERE FOR USE MADE.
WHAT'S A SUNDIAL IN THE SHADE?**

—Benjamin Franklin

A Sundial in the Shade

A sundial tells the time by casting a shadow across its face; the shadow points to a particular hour. Direct sunlight is an absolute necessity for a sundial to function; if it is in the shade, it won't work. But it would be a mistake to think that the sundial was broken and an even bigger mistake to try to fix it. In fact, any attempt to fix the sundial will probably damage it. The sundial is simply in the wrong spot and needs to be moved into the sun.

Many of us are sundials in the shade. Things aren't working, but we are not broken. We are just in the wrong spot. We need to move out of the shade and into the sun, or we need to start chopping down trees.

We've all heard the maxim "Bloom where you're planted." This is bad advice, because we aren't plants. We aren't rooted to a single spot. We have the ability to move, and we should take advantage of that. And even if we were plants, this is still bad advice. If a plant is in the wrong spot, it won't bloom at all. Trees, flowers, and other vegetation illustrate the importance of our environment. If it's too hot, too cold, too bright, or too dark, a plant can't survive. There's nothing wrong with the plant; the problem is the plant's location. Plants thrive when their environment matches their unique needs and characteristics. The same is true for us. I think it is better advice to "plant yourself where you can bloom."

THE FIRST ESSENTIAL IN A BOY'S CAREER IS TO FIND OUT WHAT HE'S FITTED FOR, WHAT HE'S MOST CAPABLE OF DOING AND DOING WITH A RELISH.

—Charles M. Schwab, cofounder of the
Bethlehem Steel Corporation

Michael Jordan was one of the greatest basketball players of all time, but then he retired and began a new career in baseball. He failed in this new pursuit and couldn't even make it out of the minor leagues. Following this failure, he returned to basketball and won three more NBA championships. Jordan's experience shows that greatness in one area doesn't necessarily generalize to other situations. A great champion in one sport was a complete failure in another.

I THINK NORMALITY IS WHATEVER THE MAJORITY DECIDES IT WILL BE, AND IN OUR COMPANY PEOPLE WITH AUTISM ARE THE NORM.

—Thorkil Sonne, founder of Specialisterne

Thorkil Sonne is the founder of Specialisterne, a Danish software-testing company. He started the company because his son has autism, and Sonne wanted him to have a meaningful job. Nearly 75 percent of the company's employees have some form of autism, but Sonne doesn't hire them because he's trying to be charitable. He hires them because their disability is the perfect fit for the work his company does.

Sonne explains that his "ambition was to use the autism characteristics as a competitive advantage." His company's work matches the unique skill sets of people with autism spectrum disorders with a major demand in the field of software and game testing. Symptoms of autism include intense focus, high tolerance for repetition, and a strong memory. These are the same skills that are necessary to be effective as a software tester. When people with autism work at Specialisterne, they're not disabled; they're uniquely qualified. SAP, the global software giant, was so impressed with Specialisterne's success that it is now looking for hundreds of people with autism to work as software testers.

Clay Marzo is the youngest surfer to ever score a perfect ten in competition. He's so good that his fellow surfers describe him as "freaky," and they mean that as a compliment. Clay also has Asperger's syndrome, a form of autism that causes him to struggle in social situations.

After years of trying to discover what was wrong with Clay, his mom gave up on having him tested for disorders and decided that "Clay is Clay." Unfortunately, other people weren't as accepting. When he wouldn't conform, people tried to make him fit in. One sponsor even dropped him because of his unusual behavior. Because he's different, Marzo has been called "rude, lazy, dumb, and shy." It is hard for people to see the positive side of his disability.

But, as an ESPN interview explained, Marzo is "not a great surfer in spite of his medical condition, but rather, because of it." People with Asperger's have a tremendous ability to focus on one thing to the exclusion of everything else. This tunnel vision has helped Marzo to excel at surfing. He might be uncomfortable interacting with people, but "in the water, there are no limits." He's found the right fit for his unique characteristics.

> **MY OBJECT IN LIVING IS TO UNITE MY AVOCATION AND MY VOCATION.**
>
> —Robert Frost, *Two Tramps in Mud Time*

Four Elements of Fit

There are four elements of finding the right fit.

The first is *passion*. What do you love? What energizes and inspires you?

The second is *proficiency*. What are your skills? Where do you excel?

The third is *payment*. How can you get compensated for activities that combine your passion and proficiency? How can you make a living doing what you love?

The final component is *purpose*. How can you make a difference? How can you make a positive contribution?

It is possible to design a meaningful and fulfilling career that includes all of these elements, but the sequence of the four elements is important. Most people address them in the wrong order. They start with payment: *How can I make the most money?* Then they move on to proficiency: *Can I do it?* This is followed by passion: *Can I tolerate the job requirements?* Finally, some consider the question of purpose: *Will this activity cause anyone harm?* Unfortunately, this approach usually leads to frustration and failure. Passion comes first.

Passion

Sometimes pursuing our passion allows us to discover unexpected ways to get paid to do what we love. Matt Harding loved to travel so he saved up, quit his job, and took a trip around the world. He recorded his trip by filming himself dancing at many of the famous locations he visited, such as Machu Picchu, Easter Island, and underwater at the Great Barrier Reef. The YouTube video of his dances went viral, eventually capturing more than thirty-three million views.

Because of Harding's tremendous popularity, he gained the sponsorship of Stride gum, allowing him to travel the world again. This time, he created another dancing video while traveling to forty-two countries over the course of fourteen months. Harding also starred in Visa's "Travel Happy" campaign and has appeared on *Good Morning America* and numerous other media outlets.

FAMOUS FREAK: Will Shortz

I was flipping through the channels the other night and got distracted by my laptop. When I looked up, I realized that I'd inadvertently stopped on C-SPAN, which was televising a graduation ceremony at Indiana University. The commencement speaker was Will Shortz, editor of the crossword puzzle for the New York Times.

I thought Shortz was joking when he said that he had a degree in enigmatology. He wasn't. Apparently, he is the only person on Earth who holds a degree in the study of puzzles. He went on to say, "What I've always enjoyed most was making and solving puzzles ... In eighth grade, when I was asked what I wanted to do with my life, I wrote 'professional puzzle maker.' The problem was a career in puzzles didn't seem possible because puzzles typically don't pay much."

When Shortz asked a well-known puzzle designer about pursuing a career in puzzling, he was told, "Don't do it. There's no money in it. You'll starve." Shortz continued his speech. "Fortunately, I didn't give up my dream ... My advice for you is, first, figure out what you enjoy doing most in life and then try to do it full-time. Life is short. Follow your passion. Don't get stuck doing something you don't enjoy." Will's experience shows that payment follows passion, not the other way around.

Purpose

Tad Agoglia owned a very successful crane company that made him into a millionaire, but he wanted more than money. He wanted meaning. So he started First Response Team of America, a nonprofit emergency management team. They track weather patterns and move quickly to the scene of floods, tornadoes, and hurricanes. Agoglia uses his past experience by bringing heavy equipment, satellite communications, and generators to communities that have been devastated. In 2008, he was chosen as one of CNN's Heroes. It might seem unusual for someone to find purpose as a crane operator, but as Agoglia explains, "we all have something to give."

Scott Harrison was an event planner. He made a lot of money and had a lot of fun organizing parties for rich and famous people and for the companies that sponsored him. Unfortunately, his success wasn't making him happy. He wanted to do something that mattered. After a trip to Africa, he started charity: water, a nonprofit organization that provides wells to communities throughout the world. Harrison now uses his marketing skills and his connections with influential people to promote a cause that saves people's lives. He has combined passion, purpose, proficiency, and payment.

Three Pepperdine University graduates, Mike Marriner, Brian McAllister, and Nathan Gebhard, were unsure what to do for a living. So they started accepting every credit card offer that they got in the mail, packed up an old RV, and traveled across the country on a road trip. What made their trip unique was that they stopped along the way to interview people who were successful and passionate about their work. The group's first interviews included Michael Dell, Sandra Day O'Connor, and Manny the Lobsterman.

Marriner, McAllister, and Gebhard filmed each of these extraordinary encounters, and this led to the birth of *Roadtrip Nation*. Interviews from the first trip became a documentary on PBS, a DVD, and a book, *Finding the Open Road*. The three founders then created an organization that allows other students to travel the country and interview inspiring people. The trio started by searching for their own road, and now they are helping other people do the same. A new, nonprofit arm of their organization is helping high school students discover their unique paths. Mike, Brian, and Nathan found their purpose in helping other people to find their purpose.

Alignment is important, but you can't spend more time doing the right things until you stop doing the wrong things. Avoidance is the next step to improving the connection between who you are and what you do.

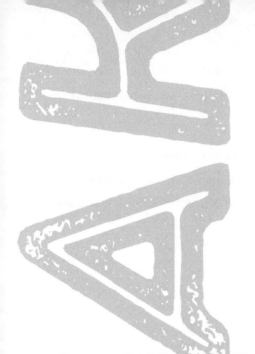

6. AVOIDANCE

• •

**YOU REALLY CAN'T TRY TO DO EVERYTHING, ESPECIALLY
IF YOU INTEND TO BE THE BEST IN THE WORLD.**

—Seth Godin, *The Dip*

Allergies

As I was boarding a plane recently, an attendant announced that we were not allowed to open or eat any products containing peanuts on the flight and that the airline would not be serving peanuts as a snack. Apparently, a passenger had a peanut allergy, and the airline didn't want to take any chances. This seemed like an extreme approach, but it was a good illustration of why avoidance works.

I think we are allergic to our weaknesses. Allergies and weaknesses are similar in a few ways. First, like allergies, we don't choose our weaknesses. They are natural. Second, you can't eliminate an allergy. Even medication just reduces the symptoms. There is no cure. Third, as we see in the airplane anecdote, the obvious solution to an allergy is to avoid whatever you are allergic to. If you're allergic to peanuts, then stay away from peanuts. If disorganization is a weakness, avoid tasks that require you to be organized. If creativity is a weakness, avoid activities that require it.

Fourth, positive thinking has no effect on allergies. It doesn't matter if you wish that you weren't allergic to peanuts or pretend that you're not; a peanut will still cause a horrible allergic reaction in your body. This is also true for weaknesses. No amount of wishful thinking will change the fact that you don't excel in this particular area. Don't sacrifice your happiness or success by continuing to attempt activities that involve your weaknesses. Treat them like bees, peanuts, dust, or pollen. Avoid them at all costs.

Fifth, even if you are allergic to several things, there are millions of things that you aren't allergic to. Life will be far more enjoyable and productive if you spend your time and energy focused on the items that don't cause problems for you. Similarly, it is more effective to focus on areas of strength than to lament your areas of weakness.

WE HAVE TO KNOW "THE NECESSARY LIMITATIONS OF OUR NATURE BEYOND WHICH WE CANNOT TRESPASS WITH IMPUNITY."

—W. H. Auden

Limitation

All this talk of avoidance can seem quite limiting. However, limitations can actually help us succeed. Barry Schwartz, in his book *The Paradox of Choice*, explains that when we have too many choices, we struggle to make decisions. He encourages us to "learn to love constraints," because "as the number of choices we face increases, freedom of choice becomes a tyranny of choice. Routine decisions take so much time and attention that it becomes difficult to get through the day. In circumstances like this, we should learn to view limits on the possibilities that we face as liberating not constraining."

Surprisingly, more options don't liberate us; they paralyze us. As Erich Fromm explained in *Escape from Freedom*, "people are beset not by a lack of opportunity but by a dizzying abundance of it." It is counterintuitive, but limitations, not options, are what liberate us.

Similarly, in his book *Predictably Irrational*, behavioral economist Dan Ariely argues that the common strategy of "keeping our options open" is a bad one and that we should "consciously start closing" some of those options. This is because "they draw energy and commitment" away from activities that promise greater success.

Erik Weihenmayer is the first and only blind man to reach the summit of Mount Everest. When asked if everything was possible, Weihenmayer answered, "No, there are limits. I mean, I can't drive a car. But there are good questions and bad questions in life. The bad questions are what-if questions. What if I were smarter or stronger? What if I could see? Those are dead-end questions. A good question is, 'how do I do as much as I can with what I have?'" Similarly, John Wooden, the most successful college basketball coach in history, said, "Do not let what you cannot do interfere with what you can do."

Our weaknesses and limitations are not a bad thing, because they rule out options for us and make it easier to focus on the areas where we can be truly successful. Limitations are liberating.

DON'T PUT OFF UNTIL TOMORROW WHAT YOU CAN PUT OFF UNTIL THE DAY AFTER TOMORROW AND END UP JUST AS WELL.

—Mark Twain

Permanent Procrastination

The majority of my students and seminar participants believe that they have a problem with procrastination, and many people cite procrastination as their primary weakness. In fact, in most classes, every student admits to having a problem in this area. Books, articles, seminars, and blog posts on overcoming procrastination are universally popular. Unfortunately, they don't work. People keep procrastinating. They can't help it. Why is it such a problem? Maybe it's not.

WHEN I'M NOT DOING SOMETHING THAT COMES DEEPLY FROM ME, I GET BORED. WHEN I GET BORED, I GET DISTRACTED, AND WHEN I GET DISTRACTED, I BECOME DEPRESSED. IT'S A NATURAL RESISTANCE, AND IT ENSURES YOUR INTEGRITY.

—María Irene Fornés

Think of the activities that you really enjoy. These might include watching movies, golfing, or shopping. Have you ever procrastinated on these activities? Probably not. You don't procrastinate on activities that you enjoy; you procrastinate on activities that you don't enjoy and don't do well. Procrastination is an important clue that there is something you dislike about the activity you are avoiding, and your distaste is a sure sign that you are dealing with an area of weakness. You wait to do these tasks until it is absolutely necessary, because you'd rather be doing something else.

PROCRASTINATION ISN'T THE PROBLEM, IT'S THE SOLUTION. SO PROCRASTINATE NOW, DON'T PUT IT OFF.

—Ellen DeGeneres

Procrastination is good. Procrastination is like a giant neon sign saying, "This is not your thing." It is a signal that you have wandered away from your strengths, that you have strayed from those activities where you can have tremendous success. I don't want you to stop procrastinating. Instead of procrastinating less, I think you should actually procrastinate more. In fact, you should stop doing those activities altogether. I'd really like to see you procrastinate permanently.

The cure for procrastination is to simply stop doing activities that you dislike. However, this certainly seems like an unrealistic suggestion, and I'll spend the rest of the chapter providing support for this unconventional strategy.

Be the Worst

Conventional wisdom says that we need to be balanced and well-rounded, and we need to be strong in all areas in order to succeed. However, that isn't true. In fact, in order to be the best in one area, you have to be willing to be the worst in others.

For example, while I was writing this book, Anthony Kim won the Shell Houston Open on the PGA Tour even though he had the worst driving accuracy of any golfer in the tournament. He wasn't just below average; he was the absolute worst.

Similarly, the two teams in the 2010 Super Bowl were the Indianapolis Colts and the New Orleans Saints. The Colts had the worst running game of any team in the NFL, and the Saints had one of the worst defenses. However, the Colts also had one of the best passing offenses, and the Saints made up for their poor defense with a league-leading offense. Both teams were the best in one area and the worst in another. In 2014, the Seattle

Seahawks won the Super Bowl. That same season, they were the most penalized team in the league.

Shaquille O'Neal is more than seven feet tall, weighs over three hundred pounds, and has missed more free throws than any other player in the history of the NBA. Because of this weakness, he has spent endless hours working with coaches to improve his skills. He is still terrible.

Shaq is so bad at free throws that other teams developed a strategy for capitalizing on his weakness. They called it Hack-a-Shaq. They would foul him before he had the opportunity to shoot so that he would have to score his points from the free-throw line.

Since other teams implemented this strategy, O'Neal has led two different teams (the Los Angeles Lakers and the Miami Heat) to four NBA championships and has been an All-Star in each year of his career. In other words, O'Neal is one of the best basketball players of all time, even though he is one of the worst free-throw shooters of all time. Another player holds the record for the lowest free-throw percentage, however. His name is Wilt Chamberlain, and he's considered by many to be the greatest player in NBA history.

O'Neal's gigantic hands make it very difficult for him to shoot effectively. However, his tremendous size also allows him to physically dominate and intimidate other players on offense and to block shots and get rebounds on defense. He is good at basketball because he is so big. He's also bad at free throws because he is so big. What makes him the best is also what makes him the worst. Similarly, if we want to be the best in one area, we need to allow ourselves to be the worst in other areas.

Twenty-two-year-old Matthias Schlitte offers an even more interesting example of this principle. He began practicing arm wrestling when he was sixteen years old, but he has only been training the muscles in his right arm. When you see a picture of him, it looks like he has some sort of genetic deformity. Schlitte's right arm is nearly eighteen inches around, but his left forearm measures only six inches. It seems like the only muscles that he has are in his right arm.

Schlitte's unusual musculature is a huge advantage in arm wrestling, because his opponents are determined by weight class. His wrestling arm is much larger than those of his competitors, because they have bodies with normal proportions. Unfortunately for them, this means that much of their weight is in parts of their bodies that don't help them with arm wrestling.

Schlitte can spend additional time and energy exercising his right arm because he doesn't have to bother with building the rest of his body. He is weak in many areas so that he can be incredibly strong in the area that is the most important. This makes him unbalanced, but it also makes him successful.

You'll never become the best by fixing your weaknesses. Excellence requires you to amplify your strengths and allow your weaknesses to get even worse.

Be Lazy

It is possible to do less and achieve more. Many people are suspicious of a "work smarter, not harder" philosophy. However, the fact is that some activities simply have more value and will provide a greater return on your investment than others.

TO FULFILL SOME COMMITMENTS, OTHERS MUST BE EXCLUDED.

—Chris Guillebeau, *The Art of Non-Conformity*

The advice to simply stop doing things you don't like might sound unreasonable, but that is because it is unconventional. Marcus Buckingham, author of *The One Thing You Need to Know*, argues that the most important thing to know about personal success is "if you don't like it, stop doing it." Management guru Peter Drucker calls this "organized abandonment," and Chris Guillebeau, author of *The Art of Non-Conformity*, refers to it as "radical exclusion." Tom Peters recommends that you go a step further and get a "stop counselor" to help you eliminate unnecessary or distracting tasks. Wine guru and speaker Gary Vaynerchuk exhorts his audiences to "stop doing what you hate!"

A couple years ago I saw Jim Collins, author of *Good to Great*, speak at the Catalyst Conference in Atlanta. One of his primary suggestions was to create a stop-doing list. Good people and good companies have to-do lists, but the best also have lists of what they will stop doing. Activities that are merely good distract us from what is best. We need to systematically eliminate these things from our lives.

Collins argued that the time we have is finite, but the number of choices we have is infinite. Therefore, it is vital to choose precisely how to make the most of the limited time that we have.

Below are a few suggestions, from Collins's website, for how to get started with your stop-doing list:

→ **Start an actual, physical list of things to stop doing.**

→ **Every time you add a new activity to your to-do list, select an activity to stop doing.**

→ **Rank each of your activities from most important to least important. Drop the bottom 20 percent of activities.**

→ **The blank page test: If an activity wasn't already on your list, would you add it now? If not, drop it.**

→ **Don't devote financial, psychological, or emotional resources to activities that don't meet the preceding criteria.**

Pruning

As a transplant to the South, I am enjoying the many new types of foliage. After several years, I am still amazed to see flowers bloom on bushes in early January. One very popular southern tree is the crepe myrtle, which caught my attention because of the way it is pruned. In the winter, you can see rows and rows of trees that have been cut back severely, with only the largest branches remaining. This annual pruning maintains the health and appearance of the tree.

TRULY SUCCESSFUL PEOPLE, THOSE WHO ENJOY EVERY PART OF THEIR LIFE AND HAVE FINANCIAL STABILITY, ARE VERY PICKY ABOUT WHERE THEY SPEND THEIR TIME AND ENERGY. SO PRUNE RELENTLESSLY.

—Pam Slim

I think it is the same for our lives. In our efforts to be well-rounded and multifaceted, we often develop branches that are unproductive. Unfortunately, we don't prune them, and they end up sapping our strength. We all have a limited amount of time, energy, and resources. Seasonal pruning keeps us from wasting those precious resources and, instead, allows us to focus on the areas with the most potential.

But if you stop doing all the things that you don't like to do, how will they get done? That's a good question, and the answer is in the next chapter: affiliation.

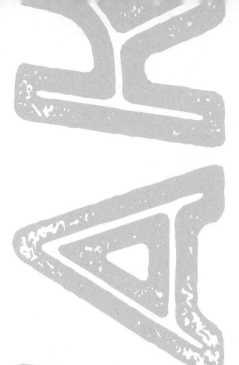

7. AFFILIATION

· ·

I GET BY WITH A LITTLE HELP FROM MY FRIENDS.

—The Beatles

If you stop doing the things you don't like to do, as I suggested in the last chapter, how will they get done? One option is to form relationships with people who have strengths that complement your weaknesses. You don't need to be well-rounded, but you can still live a balanced life by finding the right people to help you.

Many people cite complementary partnerships as an essential component of their success. Microsoft's Bill Gates and Steve Ballmer are one example of this phenomenon. However, close partnerships aren't the only way to minimize the impact of your weaknesses. Just as companies outsource aspects of their operations, you too can hire others to do tasks that you don't like or don't do well. In doing so, you'll have more time and more energy for the work that you do best.

One of my favorite examples of affiliation came from Sara Dunnigan, executive director of the Virginia Board of Workforce Development:

> I've been struggling for weeks to write an annual report for a business program that I manage. Each year, we interview about 600 business people in an effort to connect them with resources and support the growth of their businesses. The annual report is an aggregate view of the data points and every time I tried to write an engaging, conversational report that people would actually want to read—it came out like a dry article from an economic journal. While well-written and chock full of facts and figures—this was not the effect I was going for.
>
> This wasn't the first time I struggled with this project. It has been my responsibility for more than three years and

no matter what I did to get better (I must have read every other similar publication in the country) I just couldn't get there. In fact, during the time I spent trying to write, all I really wanted to do was go out and talk to stakeholders in the community about what we had discovered, what we had done and exciting plans for the future.

After struggling to write the report on her own for years, she finally tried a different approach:

I had been working with Grace, an intern in our office who was a fantastic writer. I did the data gathering and roughed in the outline and she reorganized the content and added the dimensional writing I was looking for in the project. I'm happy because now I get to focus on building on my skills as a speaker and solutions facilitator and Grace got to use her skills and add another great project to her portfolio. Now I am excited about using this approach for other projects our small team works on.

Finding someone else to write the report was a win-win-win situation. Sara was happy because she had more time to do what she loved. Her company and constituents were happy because the report was more interesting, and Grace was happy because she had an opportunity to use her strengths at work. Affiliation enhances teamwork and improves performance.

Don't Do It Yourself

Based on the popularity of the DIY Network, it seems that Americans love to do things themselves. Every weekend, people overcome the temptation to hire qualified and experienced craftsmen to complete a plumbing, electrical, and carpentry project and instead choose to do it themselves. It is an understandable impulse; it costs a lot to pay someone else to do the work. It is much cheaper to just do it yourself. Or so it seems.

I believe that the only reason it seems cheaper to do things ourselves is because we don't really calculate the costs. We calculate the cost of the materials but not the cost of our time. We also fail to count the cost of the opportunities that we miss while we are studying the subtleties of begonia fertilizer.

Economists refer to this as *opportunity cost*, which means that some activities are mutually exclusive. You want to do two things, but you can't do them both. Pam Slim calls this *displacement*, which means that "everything that you do rules out something else that you can't do." Choosing one activity eliminates the possibility of doing the other activity. The opportunity cost is the price that you pay for missing out on the other option. This cost can be time, energy, money, or anything else that you value.

If you've ever paid an ATM fee for withdrawing your money from another bank, then you understand opportunity cost. You could have driven across town to your bank and withdrawn the money without paying a fee, but you decided that you'd rather spend the money on the fee than spend the time driving. You sacrificed your money in order to save time.

There are other issues to consider as well. Is it really cheaper to do something yourself if you include your hourly rate in the cost? Although you might earn less per hour than the plumber, it will surely take you longer to complete the same task. The task may also require you to buy tools or equipment that you will probably never use again.

Consider lawn care. How much does it really cost to mow your own lawn? You have to take into consideration the cost of the mower, weed-eater, edger, spreader, blower, gas, oil, repairs, etc. If you have a riding mower, the initial investment is huge. What if you had invested that money into a good mutual fund? The earnings alone might have been enough to pay someone to cut your grass. Additionally, when working on projects that are more complex than lawn care, a competent plumber, electrician, or carpenter can probably do it better than the weekend amateur. What will it cost if you do it wrong?

I think it is even more important to consider what you could be doing instead of doing it yourself. Instead of learning a little bit about something that you'll never do again, you could be increasing your expertise in a more relevant area. You could earn more if you got more education or earned additional certifications. You could read a good book about your industry or profession. What is the long-term financial cost of missing out on all these opportunities while you are learning to install replacement windows?

Instead of making friends with the clerk at the hardware store, you could be building relationships with your children or spouse. What are those relationships worth? It will certainly cost you more in the future if you don't build and maintain those relationships now.

Similarly, time spent trying to fix your weaknesses or forcing yourself to fit in takes away from time you could have spent building on your strengths (amplification) or finding the right fit (alignment). We want to do it all, but we can't (avoidance).

Outsourcing

We already outsource many life activities because we recognize that it isn't worth our time to complete them or that they can be done better by someone else. Throughout history, the following tasks consumed almost every second of every day for most people:

→ Growing food

→ Harvesting food

→ Cooking food

→ Making fabric

→ Sewing clothes

→ Building houses

→ Manufacturing vehicles

These may seem like obvious examples, but they illustrate the wisdom of outsourcing. We just haven't taken it far enough. We have many more opportunities to stop doing things ourselves.

→ Stop changing your oil or doing any vehicle maintenance—go to Jiffy Lube.

→ Stop washing your car—take it to a car wash.

→ Stop cleaning your house—hire Merry Maids.

→ Stop doing your taxes—find a good accountant or use H&R Block.

→ Stop managing your own investments— find a local independent advisor.

→ Stop mowing your grass—pay a neighborhood kid to do it or make your kids do it.

Add up how much time you would save each week if you stopped doing these activities. Then, start a new list. What could you do instead? How could you invest your time and energy so that they will pay off over the long term? Here are some ideas:

→ Start your own business.

→ Go back to school.

→ Spend more time with your kids.

→ Attend a seminar.

→ Start a blog.

→ Read a good book.

→ Start exercising.

→ Write a book.

→ Volunteer.

Some of these suggestions might seem small, but I know from personal experience that eliminating low-leverage tasks to make room for high-leverage activities can create big breakthroughs. I hate any kind of routine maintenance activities, and mowing the lawn is one of the worst. As soon as I'm done cutting the grass, it just starts growing right back. My wife would always complain because I waited too long and let the grass get too tall. Our new yard in North Carolina was huge, and it took almost three hours each week to take care of it. During the middle of the summer, it was even worse. It needed to be mowed every five days instead of just once a week.

I had a decision to make. I wanted my wife to have a nice yard, but I also wanted to spend time with my wife and kids and start my own business. I couldn't do it all. I didn't have enough time.

So I decided to hire the neighbor's son to mow the grass. I paid him $20, which was about $7 per hour. Then I took the three hours that I was spending on the lawn and dedicated it to my business. I purchased a website address and hired my friend to create a website. My father-in-law, who is a graphic designer, helped me create business cards. I started going to events at the local chamber of commerce and began work on my first book. It wasn't much: just three hours a week. But it was enough to create momentum and allow me to still do the other things that were really important to me.

It's been eleven years since I started my business, and each year has been more successful than the last. I've certainly made more than enough money to pay someone to handle our landscaping needs. But I never would have had any of this success if I was still mowing my own grass.

I'd encourage you to start by outsourcing the tasks that you dislike the most. They probably aren't a good fit for you, and they cost you time, energy, and stress. Once you pay to save yourself some time, invest the time in an activity that you are good at and that you enjoy. You'll be rewarded with additional energy, fulfillment, and confidence, which will directly or indirectly lead to more money in the future.

One objection that I usually get to outsourcing is that people can't afford it. This is a "chicken or the egg" argument. My point is that the only way to improve your current financial situation is to stop doing those things that distract you from doing what you do best. It will pay off in the long run.

Now that I'm self-employed, I'm a free agent, but there are a lot of skills that I don't have and don't want to learn. I want to stay focused on the things that I do best: speaking and writing. In order to do this, I outsource almost every aspect of my business. Eric Smoldt at Group 3 does all my graphic design. Mark Novelli helps me with website design. John Bly at LB&A handles my accounting and taxes. Amazon.com handles the processing and shipping for all my products. Advantage Media publishes my books.

Outsourcing is just one way to take care of things that you don't like. You can also partner with family members, friends, coworkers, and people in your community, although there are two barriers to doing so. First, we believe that no one wants to do the tasks that we dislike. Second, we want other people to accept our weaknesses, but we don't want to accept their flaws.

Dirty Jobs

One of the problems with finding people to do tasks that we find distasteful is that we believe that the task itself is inherently disagreeable. We tell ourselves that nobody wants to do it and that nobody likes it. But that's not true.

There is almost always someone who loves to do what you hate to do. He or she loves the task for the same reason that you hate it. For example, you hate repetition. It bores you. But there is someone else that loves the routine and certainty of repetitive tasks. It soothes them.

Dirty Jobs, the popular TV show starring Mike Rowe, profiles people involved in all sorts of objectionable tasks like cleaning portable toilets, raising turkeys, treating sewage, repairing giant tires, or making bricks. But the show proves the adage that "one man's trash is another man's treasure." Although these jobs seem disgusting, the people who do them usually seem to be enjoying themselves. There is something about the jobs that they like. Maybe they want to be outside, work with their hands, be alone, or see the finished product.

Symbiosis

Symbiosis is a mutually beneficial relationship between organisms with differing abilities and needs. In other words, a symbiotic relationship is one in which two parties help each other by providing something that the other party needs but can't provide for themselves.

For example, the Nile crocodile can't clean its own teeth. The Egyptian plover, a bird, helps the crocodile by walking around in its mouth and picking food and other debris out of the crocodile's teeth. The crocodile could easily crush the bird and swallow it whole. But it doesn't, because the bird provides a needed service. The plover gets a free meal and the protection of a fearsome predator, and the crocodile gets free dental care. Symbiosis is the essence of affiliation.

Imperfect People

We all want to be accepted for who we are. We want people to accept our quirks and limitations. Unfortunately, we are often unwilling to do this for others. *The Freak Factor* isn't just about you, your weaknesses, and their corresponding strengths. It is also about the people around you: your coworkers, family, and friends.

If affiliation is so effective, then why aren't more people doing it? The answer is simple. The people we need the most are often the people we like the least. When someone has a strength we don't have, we fail to see it and see the corresponding weakness instead. For example, if I'm an inspiring and visionary leader who isn't good at implementation and organization, I need a business partner, COO, or assistant who is good at these things. But instead of seeing those people as detail-oriented and meticulous, I will tend to see them as small-minded, petty, perfectionistic, and compulsive. I'll also complain that they are not as visionary as I am, that they don't have my essential strengths, and that they are worse than me in every way.

In order to benefit from affiliation, we need to reframe the characteristics of others to look for the strength in every weakness. What bothers you most about the people in your life? Try to find the strength that corresponds with their most obvious weaknesses, and then go one step further. Don't just tolerate their uniqueness, encourage them to flaunt it. If you do this, you will see a dramatic improvement in your relationships, and people will probably respond differently to your freakiness as well. Differentiation requires you to be unique, and that often means accepting and encouraging imperfection in yourself and others.

For example, Tom Peters wrote an interesting blog post about the value of people who do the last two percent of a task. These are the people who make sure it is just right; the people who take care of the seemingly minor details; the people who ensure that everything is perfect before a presentation is made or a project is submitted.

In the last few lines, Peters says, "sometimes we call the last two-percenter a 'pain in the ass.' True, but no one is of greater importance to the success of what we do." Are you a "two-percenter?" If you aren't a two-percenter, consider the possibility that the pain caused by these people is a small price to pay for the value they deliver. If we want other people to accept our freak factors, we need to be willing to accept theirs as well.

I downloaded the new Pearl Jam album *Backspacer* from iTunes, and it included a short video about the band. The following quote from one of the band members caught my attention. "We sort of have our own thing and it's raw and it's an imperfect combination of personalities and we put a lot of faith in

Ed (Eddie Vedder) as the artistic director to take bits and pieces from everybody and, in the end, he ties us together."

Sometimes we believe that success requires a perfect combination of personalities, but the enduring success of Pearl Jam demonstrates that our imperfections can be combined to create something incredible. We need to acknowledge and accept people's imperfections and then tie them all together in a unique way. We need to stop looking for perfect people to partner with and start working with the imperfect people whom we already know. We need to be the artistic directors of our own lives.

Affiliation isn't just about finding people who are strong where you are weak; it is also about finding people who like you just the way you are. It is about finding your community, finding your people—fellow freaks.

Choose Your Audience

"Know your audience" is the conventional wisdom for speakers. If you know your audience, you can adapt the message to fit their particular needs. For example, giving a presentation to a kindergarten class is a lot different than giving a keynote speech to five hundred managers.

There is some truth to this wisdom, but it assumes that you have the ability to make this adjustment. Intellectually, I know that I can't talk to kindergarteners the same way that I talk to adults, but that doesn't mean I have the skill to capture the attention of the five-year-olds. Knowing your audience and being able to give them what they want are two different things.

Furthermore, there are some people who just aren't interested in what you have to say. No amount of effort will change that. I once did a presentation on how nonprofits earn money to support their missions by starting businesses that sell products and services. One of the women in the audience worked for an anticapitalistic (antibusiness) activist organization. I'm not sure why she chose to attend, but there was nothing that I was going to say that would fit with her perspective.

That is why instead of knowing your audience, you should choose your audience. Instead of adapting your message to the audience, you should find the right audience for your message. You should find out who your ideal audience is and who is open to your message. Find out who is attracted to your approach and perspective, and then communicate with those people.

THERE'S A MESSAGE FOR EVERY AUDIENCE AND AN AUDIENCE FOR EVERY MESSAGE.

—Olalah Njenga

Larry the Cable Guy, a comedian on the Blue Collar Comedy Tour, is obnoxious, immature, gross, and prejudiced. Many people find his act incredibly offensive. But when tickets go on sale for his show, they usually sell out. In one night, he earns $250,000 even though a lot of people haven't heard of or don't like him.

Larry chooses his audience, and they choose him. He doesn't try to convert people who don't like him, and he doesn't try to adapt his style to make everyone happy. He seeks out people who enjoy his brand of comedy and gives them what they want.

Pam Slim believes that it is important for each of us to find our people. "These are not just those people who would grudgingly fork over money for your product or service; they are people who would clamor to do business with you because you are the exact answer to their problems. They are your ideal partners, clients, customers, and mentors. These are people whom you like to spend time with, who embrace you despite your perceived warts, mistakes, and flaws, and who are deeply affected by your work."

The right people will not reject you for being yourself or for being real. Don't try to please everyone. Try to please the right people.

TO SUCCEED, YOU MUST DELEGATE EVERYTHING EXCEPT THAT WHICH IS YOUR GENIUS WORK.

—Fabienne Fredrickson

FREAK PROFILE: Jennifer Schuchmann

Jennifer Schuchmann (pronounced shook-man) is a writer from Atlanta. In addition to writing, she leads workshops for aspiring writers. But she has two big weaknesses. First, she doesn't have a lot of original ideas, which makes it difficult to come up with something to write about. Second, she isn't good with spelling and grammar, which are seemingly vital skills for a writer. So, how did her book, *First Things First*, end up on the *New York Times* best seller list? I'll let Jennifer tell you in her own words.

"I have a very hard time coming up with ideas. I respond well to specifics, tell me you need a paragraph about how to make furniture from nuts and I can think of 80 things to say. Tell me to write about whatever I want and I can't think of a thing."

Because of this, Schuchmann thought, "I could never be a writer. Spelling and diagramming sentences just didn't interest me. I could look at the same sentence ... and not see the mistakes. My brain just didn't focus on that. So in high school, I stopped writing. I realized I apparently didn't have what it takes to be a writer. I didn't have ideas and I didn't have the technical skills 'good writers' had." But then she had an epiphany.

> I was in a workshop listening to a publisher talk about how writers are in love with their own words. I thought to myself, "I'm not." From that moment I realized that I was different from the other writers I had met in the past. I realized that I was a writer who takes assignments. There are stories or articles that need to be told, and writers who are too passionate about their own ideas [and who] can't write those stories, but I could.
>
> Now less than ten years later, I've already published five books, all collaborations with other people. My latest book, *First Things First*, with Kurt and Brenda Warner was an assignment to write 75,000 words in 19 days. The book is now out, and yesterday was number ten on the *New York Times* best seller list for hardcover nonfiction.
>
> What has changed? Well, I've learned to embrace the fact that I can get behind other people's ideas, that not having my own isn't a hindrance to being a writer. And in the case of being a collaborative writer, not being married to my own ideas is a really good thing. My agent continues to remind

me that the ability to write fast is a unique skill. I've learned to compensate for misspellings or verbs that don't agree by hiring an outside editor or other writer who has those skills to look through my manuscript before I submit it.

I teach at a lot of writers' conferences and I tell my story so that writers realize they need to capitalize on their strengths and find ways to compensate for their perceived weaknesses.

Jennifer's story demonstrates the power of affiliation. She proves that it is possible to have tremendous success without fixing your weaknesses. She has succeeded by embracing her flaws, because she sees the strengths that are hiding inside them. For example, because she is not restricted by the traditional rules of spelling and grammar, she can write quickly. She deals easily with this apparent weakness by hiring people to edit her work.

Because Schuchmann is not bursting with ideas of her own, she is open to the ideas of others. She capitalizes on this weakness by helping others to tell their stories. I experienced her gift for understanding during our phone conversation. She immediately understood the freak factor and sometimes explained the concept even better than I could.

PART THREE: WORK

DIFFERENTLY

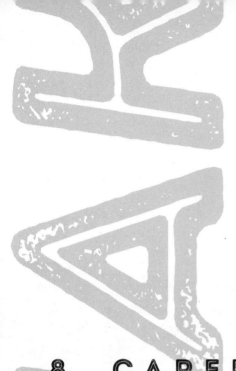

8. CAREER

· ·

MAYBE YOU NEED MORE THAN A NEW JOB;
YOU NEED A NEW LINE OF WORK.

—Marc Cullen, MD

Anna wakes up at 6 a.m. but wishes she could sleep for a few more hours. After getting the kids some breakfast and taking them to school, she drives to the office. Her job pays well, and her boss and coworkers are nice enough. But she still dreads going to work, and at the end of the day she feels drained—like the life has been sucked out of her.

Anna has put on a lot of weight over the last few years. She knows that she needs to exercise and eat better, but she doesn't have any energy left once she gets home. Her lack of energy also makes her impatient and easily irritated, which strains her relationships with her husband and children.

Anna has read books on time management, stress management, exercise, healthy eating, parenting, and marriage, but nothing seems to work. Her manager has identified a few areas of improvement on Anna's performance evaluation and has developed an action plan for her to follow. Specifically, she needs to be more flexible and work on her interpersonal skills. She has attended seminars, worked with a coach, and tried diligently to achieve the goals in the plan, but she isn't making much progress.

Anna wants to change. She wants to grow. She's motivated and focused, but it just isn't working. She finds herself asking the same questions over and over again.

→ **What's wrong with me?**

→ **What am I missing?**

→ **Why can't I make any progress?**

→ **What should I do?**

If Anna came to you for help, what would you tell her?

→ **Does she need to try harder?**

→ **Does she need to set clearer goals?**

→ **Does she need therapy?**

→ **Does she need a personal trainer or a life coach?**

→ **Should she join a support group like Weight Watchers?**

→ **Should she get a new job? If so, what kind of job should she look for?**

Before we can answer these questions, we need to go back a few years. When Anna was in school, she always got good grades. Although she wasn't the most popular girl in school, she did well in most of her classes and stayed out of trouble. Her teachers consistently commented on her shyness and encouraged her to come out of her shell. School administrators also warned her that she needed to improve her participation and performance in physical education.

Anna's parents wished that she'd spend less time in her room and more time with other kids and the family. They pushed her to join a sports team or some other extracurricular group activity. Sometimes they'd use terms like *antisocial* and wondered if she had some kind of disorder. Their fears were reinforced by Anna's desire to be in control and keep everything very organized. Since she was very little, she'd always been very neat and liked to have things in their proper places. After seeing a special news report on television, Anna's parents even wondered if she might have OCD.

In college, Anna decided to see a counselor after taking an introductory psychology class. Listening to the professor and reading the textbook convinced her that she wasn't normal and that she needed to get some help. The counselor tried to teach her how to interact more effectively with others and how to be more comfortable with her roommate's messiness. The ideas that Anna learned seemed to make sense, but they just didn't stick. She stopped going to her sessions and concluded that she must be lacking in self-discipline or motivation.

For Anna's entire life, the people around her—teachers, parents, and managers—seemed convinced that there was something wrong with her. After a while, she started to believe them. How could they all be wrong?

Your Job Is Killing You

Anna isn't alone. In talking with my seminar participants, students, friends, and family members, I've found a lot of people who are frustrated in their efforts to create the life and career that they've imagined. When I ask students what they want to change about their life, they consistently say that they want to find better jobs or start their own businesses. My experience is supported by a recent Intuit study, which showed that 72 percent of employees "dream of starting their own business" and 67 percent of respondents said that they "contemplate resigning from their job on a regular basis." Other studies show that 70 percent of employees are not motivated at work and don't even know how to do their jobs well.

According to a CNN Money report, job satisfaction in the United States hit a twenty-two-year low in 2009. The study found that more than half of American employees are frustrated by their work. "The Conference Board's survey polled 5,000 households, and found that only 45% were satisfied in their jobs. That's down from 61.1% in 1987, the first year the survey was conducted. Even though one in 10 Americans is out of a job, those who are employed are increasingly dissatisfied. 'Through both economic boom and bust during the past two decades, our job satisfaction numbers have shown a consistent downward trend,' said Lynn Franco, director of the Consumer Research Center of The Conference Board.'"[5]

These numbers are staggering! It's not just a few people who are unhappy at work—it is most people. If you like your job and do it well, you are in the minority. You are rare.

So why am I focusing on work? Why not discuss Anna's other concerns, like health, parenting, and marriage? Because I think Anna's poor health, difficult family relationships, and lack of sleep are just symptoms of an underlying problem in her career. The root of the problem is work.

As one study showed, more health issues are caused by work than by financial or family problems. A similar study revealed that 25 percent of respondents believed that their job was the biggest source of stress in their lives. This is partly due to the fact that we spend more of our waking hours at work than on any other activity. If our job is draining instead of fulfilling, it will have a dramatically negative impact on our life.

Pam Slim helps people to create alternatives to their current jobs because, in her words, "I found a lot of despair hidden

5 | http://money.cnn.com/2010/01/05/news/economy/job_satisfaction_report/

behind smiling faces of smart people in cubicles over the years. Gut wrenching, tears, confusion, sadness, anger, you name it, I heard it." According to Dan Miller, author of *48 Days to the Work You Love*, most suicides occur on Sunday nights, and most heart attacks happen on Monday mornings. Unfortunately, some people would rather die than go to work, and even if they do go to the office, the job kills them anyway.

It is no surprise, then, that one of the most popular television shows in the United Kingdom and the United States is *The Office*, which chronicles the apathy, incompetence, frustration, and futility of corporate life. Similarly, organizations throughout the world are littered with copies of Dilbert cartoons, a comic strip with themes similar to those of *The Office*. The success of Dilbert and *The Office* shows just how unhappy our companies and our employees have become. This is also why Pam Slim's book *Escape from Cubicle Nation* has become a best seller. The title of the first chapter of the book is a profound question: "I have a fancy title, steady paycheck, and good benefits. Why am I so miserable?"

One of Slim's coaching clients explained it this way. "I describe my office job and cubicle as toxic to my spirit. Before I graduated, I was ambitious, excited and had big dreams. My work sucks all the creativity and fun ... and is starting to sap my spirit too. It has dampened my will and motivation and has just made me stop caring. I'm ... no longer excited about projects or making a difference. I'm just going through the motions ... it's hard to keep the lethargic work energy from spilling over to other aspects of my life."

Why are people so frustrated with their jobs? Why do they want to start their own businesses? People are unhappy in their careers because their jobs require them to do work that drains their energy and to be strong where they are weak. A recent Gallup survey found that only 20 percent of employees feel like they have the opportunity to do what they do best every day. This means that 80 percent of employees feel trapped by work that relies on them to excel in their areas of weakness. There is a lack of alignment between what we do well and what we have to do at work.

In a *Men's Health* article, Marc Cullen, MD, a professor of medicine at Yale University, explains that "the amount of stress you feel from your job has a lot to do with whether the job fits you—that is, whether it matches your personality and style and other demands of your life ... If you come home at the end of the day feeling angry, alienated, and exhausted, maybe you need more than a new job; you need a new line of work. The biggest problems are with a misfit. If you're a misfit, fix it—or you'll die trying."

Pam Slim explains that being trapped in the wrong job can lead to the following:

→ Not being able to identify what makes you happy

→ A feeling of numbness and emptiness

→ A feeling of burning rage

→ A feeling of powerlessness and loss of self

→ A sense of loneliness

→ A loss of direction

If you're feeling this way, what should you do?

Seven Ways to Find the Right Work

The most common question that I get after my seminar is, "Do I have to quit my job to find my freak factor?" In other words, people want to flaunt their weaknesses, but they are afraid of how it will affect their existing careers and personal finances. Craig Houston has a good perspective on this question. Instead of answering it directly, he challenges people to examine the real consequences of staying in the wrong job. "Are you stuck in a job and afraid to leave because of the security it provides for your family? If the job makes you miserable, what are you really providing for your family anyway?"

Houston argues that "your energy and presence is perhaps the most significant gift you can provide (to your family). The truth is, when you have found the most fitting work, it makes you feel incredible. Would you like to feel like a rock star or superhero every day? Imagine what that would do for every aspect of your life." Chris Ferdinandi at Renegade HR argues that many potential rock stars appear to be below average or mediocre, because they're "in the wrong position that isn't well aligned with their passions and strengths." Similarly, Laurie Ruettimann says that if you've just had a less-than-positive assessment from your boss, don't freak out. Instead, "think about a new job. Think about a new career. Think about living the kind of life where it doesn't matter what your boss or supervisor thinks about you."

Below are seven options for finding or creating a better fit between your unique characteristics and your work. They are listed in order of difficulty and the degree to which they will disrupt your life. The easiest options are first, and the harder ones follow.

229

Alignment isn't an all-or-nothing proposition. Take a look at the strategies below, and start with the one that you are most comfortable with. The point is to start somewhere and start now.

1. Keep your job and pursue your passion through hobbies, volunteering, or family involvement.

If you can find positive outlets for your unique qualities, your work will seem more bearable.

> **IF YOU'RE NOT PASSIONATE ABOUT YOUR JOB,**
> **FIND WORK AWAY FROM YOUR PAID JOB**
> **THAT MAKES YOU COME ALIVE.**
>
> —Sital Ruparelia

I met Allan Bacon at a conference in North Carolina. His article "Moving to Paris without Quitting My Day Job" offers some great ideas for finding your passion by performing Life Experiments.

> When I wake up I can look through the opening in the heavy drapes and see that I am still here. Cool, it wasn't a dream. I see the 1800s Haussmann-style townhouse across the street from our Paris apartment and I hear the sounds of Vespa scooters blaring down the street and shopkeepers talking as they open for business. Then I remember that I have three weeks to go living in the leafy 16th arrondissement with my wife and three daughters—for free, without taking vacation and without quitting my job.

I couldn't have even conceived of this just three years earlier. Back then I was miserable in a corporate job.

A snapshot: one night I couldn't sleep because I was so stressed about work. So what did I do? I got up and went to work—at 4 am. When I walked into the office I expected quiet. So I was surprised when I heard the clicking of keyboards and saw the lights on in several cubicles. At this company, everyone knew the trick of sending late night emails to "prove" our value as hardworking and committed to the company. I just didn't realize so many of those emails were coming from the office.

So, how did a 40-year-old average guy find his way from wee-hours corporate email suck-up to paid Parisian expat in three years? I needed to learn three seemingly oxymoronic approaches to break the unspoken "rules" of the conformist career path.

To keep moving forward, go backward.

Why did I stay in my crazy corporate environment? Because it was so good! Seriously. I had great pay, a big bonus, growth potential and benefits. I'd have to be crazy to leave that, right? Unfortunately, it was the environment that was making me crazy—it was like I was diving without a snorkel—the harder I tried to move forward, the more stressed I got and the less I could breathe.

So what did I do? I gave up. I did the unthinkable and went backwards on the career ladder. I went back to a job at a company I had had five years previously. Now instead of just a snorkel, I felt like I had a giant air tank on my back. Everything was easier and I had much more room to think and explore other options for my career.

Surprisingly, even though I had the same job, I learned that I was not the same person. I knew more and could add more value. Within a year my salary was higher than it had been at my old job, I was making a much bigger impact and I was starting to see new possibilities for myself. I was diving deeper and seeing more fish.

To understand your passions, don't analyze, experiment.

Have you ever changed careers? The best approaches I could find used tests and coaching and analysis to help you look back at your history and then find the next step to a job that would make you happier. These never seemed to help me make the type of big change I was looking for.

It was the equivalent of trying to decide whether I would like mango ice cream by analyzing my past food choices. If I were doing it career-planning style, it would go something like this:

OK, let's look at what you've liked in the past—vanilla, strawberry—great. And let's have you fill out what tastes you like. We'll analyze these and rate you on the "Sweet/Tangy" scale. Then we'll have you read a summary of the mango flavor. OK, based on those you need to decide whether to switch over to mango from vanilla.

I needed a way to actually take a taste of the areas that might bring me more satisfaction. How could I actually try being a DJ or a professional photographer without putting my whole family at risk? And how could I do it in very little time and with almost no cost?

I needed a way to take a bite-sized taste of different parts of life. I needed to be able to do Life Experiments.

To find more satisfying work, focus on playing.

About this same time, another realization hit me. Work is a terrible place to find your calling. Just like the career tests limited me to my past work experience, my job limited me to my current role in the company. I guess I could have offered to DJ the company holiday party, but I didn't see them letting me spend four hours a week doing that.

Back when I was a kid, we didn't need to do any analysis to try something new. We just did it. When I wanted to be a radio DJ in 5th grade, I took my turntable to my friend Brian's house. With our two turntables and a microphone we mixed a complete radio show: music, jokes, call-ins and shout-outs. When we played the tape at school, my teacher snorted because she was laughing so hard.

Notice what we didn't do: we didn't just dream about being DJs and we didn't read about DJs and we didn't interview a DJ. We were DJs. As kids, there were no limits to what jobs we could "try on."

So I started doing Life Experiments by working them into the cracks and crevices of my busy schedule outside of work: visiting art galleries on a lunch break, taking photos on the weekend, exploring Tokyo paper shops between sales calls on a business trip. My guiding principle was to find the fastest, cheapest way to take action and try the essence of all the interests and job ideas I had.

All of these experiments gave me more and more ideas and more and more confidence in what was right for me. Eventually I realized that my wife and I could probably find a way to experiment with living abroad. Et voilà, Paris.

Finding Your Own "Paris."

The impact of these Life Experiments was way out of proportion to the effort. On a flight back from Asia, it hit me that the part of my job that mattered most to my company was when I was face-to-face with customers. And that it didn't really matter where my office was. So instead of taking my kids on a crazy, bleary-eyed tour across Europe, I decided that we should find a way to actually live there long enough to get a taste for what the experience would be like. Would we kill each other in a city apartment? Would we get bored? Would we go crazy from having to learn how to navigate in a place where we didn't speak the language?

Of course, none of those things happened. Our Paris trip was done by a house swap with a French family. I used Home Exchange and highly recommend it. In Paris, my daughters learned that not everyone around the world saw things the way we do, and they began imagining a whole new set of possibilities for their future. I arranged my business meetings for Europe while I was there—my company saved money and my customers were happy to have quick access to me.

The benefits impacted all aspects of my life. As I continued my Life Experiments, things started happening faster than I could have ever imagined. Each thing led to several new things. I had started my Avocationist blog about a year before I left work. The original purpose was to share helpful stories with others going through transitions. But as I interviewed people for the blog and I continued my own explorations, I realized that I needed to share the lessons I had learned with a bigger audience.

I applied one of my own big messages and made the mental shift to seeing work as a means to an end instead of the main focus on my life. I had some money saved up and then I negotiated an agreement with my employer to consult with them a day a week. This kept money coming in and gave me more time to work on speaking, writing and doing seminars. It's only one year past Paris and I'm writing a book and consulting, no longer working in a company at all.

Don't quit your job. Just quit thinking. Start experimenting. It will change your life.

2. *Keep your job and adapt your responsibilities to focus more on activities that you enjoy and do well and less on activities you dislike and do poorly.*

This step requires a good relationship with your supervisor. If you have this conversation, you need to focus on the benefits that the department and company will experience if you are allowed to adjust your role. Marcus Buckingham has a lot of wonderful examples of how this has been done effectively in his book *Go Put Your Strengths to Work.*

SUCCESS IS NOT DEFINED BY POSITION OR PAY SCALE BUT BY THIS: DOING THE MOST WHAT YOU DO BEST.

—Max Lucado

Most people don't enjoy everything about their jobs. Instead of trying to find the perfect job or business, we should strive to increase the number of hours per day when we can apply our strengths and decrease the number of hours per day that we spend in our areas of weakness. Here are seven suggestions to get you started:

Estimate the percentage of time that you spend in your areas of strength and weakness.

Is your time spent on 20 percent strength and 80 percent weakness? Is it 50 percent strength and 50 percent weakness? A student once told me that her job required her to spend just 10 percent of her time in areas of strength and 90 percent in areas of weakness.

List the specific activities that allow you to do what you do best and those that put a spotlight on your flaws.

- → What tasks do you love to do?

- → When do you lose track of time?

- → What types of work are you consistently recognized and praised for?

- → What tasks do you hate to do?

- → When does time seem to stand still?

- → What type of work do you consistently struggle with?

Schedule more activities that draw on your strengths.

- → Do you have the authority to make these decisions?

- → Do you need to involve your supervisor?

- → Do you need the cooperation of your coworkers?

Eliminate tasks that draw on your flaws.

- → Is the task essential?

- → Can you get help from someone?

- → Can you exchange tasks with a coworker who has complementary strengths?

Set a target.

If your current ratio of time spent is 20 percent strength and 80 percent weakness, then maybe 50/50 is a worthwhile goal. Even a small change in this percentage will pay large dividends in energy, motivation, and results. This, in turn, will help you to make it through the parts of your job that are less desirable.

Refuse the next promotion.

Laurence Peter is the creator of the Peter Principle, which states that "every employee tends to rise to their level of incompetence." In other words, we move up in organizations until we find ourselves unable to do the work that is required.

I think that this is true and that there is a simple explanation: people who are successful get promoted. Unfortunately, the positions that they are promoted into often require different strengths than those they possess. As they move up, they gradually move further away from the situations that made them successful and the situations that fit their unique characteristics.

The best example of the Peter Principle is the salesperson who becomes the sales manager. The strengths and corresponding weaknesses of a great salesperson aren't necessarily suited to effective management. Because of this reality, we need to be more concerned about finding the right fit than about moving up. Moving up often means moving out of our sweet spot, and it might actually undermine our long-term success.

Ask for a demotion.

This might seem like a crazy suggestion, but if being promoted is sometimes undesirable, maybe we should be looking for a demotion. Allan Bacon calls this "strategic downshifting."

A local television station in Baltimore hired a young African American woman to coanchor the evening news. Unfortunately, the station managers believed that she was too emotional and not detached enough to be a big-city news anchor. When she flubbed a line, she'd laugh. When a story was sad, she'd cry.

There were several things about her appearance the station managers didn't like, so they decided to demote her to an early morning talk show. And that morning show was the perfect fit for Oprah Winfrey's personality. Getting demoted was the best thing that ever happened to her.

3. Keep your job and start a part-time business during your evenings and weekends.

You can make a lot of progress on an entrepreneurial venture without ever quitting your job. It can also be helpful and wise to explore the viability of your business concept before giving up your full-time income. Your day job will be much more bearable if you have the hope of someday leaving to pursue your business full-time. Pam Slim's book *Escape from Cubicle Nation* is a helpful guide.

Slim cautions that even though leaving your job is risky, staying in your job isn't safe either. The current economic downturn and rising unemployment rate are painful reminders of this fact. Because of this, you need to be ready to leave your employer, especially because your employer might leave you first.

As I watched formerly high-flying corporate employees slink out of their offices with their personal effects in cardboard boxes, I asked myself: "Who feels better today, those employees who put all of their effort into their job, or those who took the time to develop a wide social network, invest in self-development, and pursue a small business on the side?"

Probably the easiest way to turn your passion into your job is to do it gradually. If possible, don't quit your day job before launching your business. If you want to podcast, start with a monthly show or with a very short weekly show and see how it works. If you want to open up a yogurt shop, take a part-time job in someone else's yogurt shop and learn everything you can about how to run the business.

If you're passionate enough, it won't even feel like work. In many cases, if your idea is a good one, you'll eventually become so busy or successful in your part-time endeavor that it will be clear when you should quit your day job and become a full-time independent business owner.

Pam Slim has ten other great suggestions for getting started without leaving your job:

1. Take responsibility for your decision to keep your job.

2.   Learn as much as you can during the workday.

3.   Look for projects that relate to your business idea.

4.   Find a mentor and/or coach.

5.   Network with other entrepreneurs
     and potential customers.

6.   Attend conferences and workshops.

7.   Take advantage of your company's
     tuition reimbursement policy.

8.   Get out of debt.

9.   Save up six months of living expenses.

10. Simplify your life and reduce
     your monthly expenses.

The last three tips related to personal finances are especially important. You're not really afraid of losing your job. You're afraid of being unable to pay your bills. By increasing your savings account and reducing debts and living expenses, you are reducing the probability that your business will fail. This is because your new business won't have to generate nearly as much profit as it would if you didn't follow these three steps. Don't make it harder than it has to be. Adjust your lifestyle, at least in the beginning, to fit your dreams of becoming an entrepreneur.

4. *Stay at your company, but request a transfer to a new job that matches your skills and interests.*

For example, maybe you're working in accounting but feel that your creativity is being stifled by all the rules and regulations, and your innovative ideas are seen as dangerous and unwise. A transfer to the marketing department or to a new-program-development position might change people's perceptions of the value that you bring to the company and give you a greater sense of fulfillment as well.

Kate took this approach, and it worked for her. "I have been contemplating applying for a different position at work. After I read your *Freak Factor* manifesto, a coworker stopped me in the hallway and encouraged me to consider it. And I thought that it would be wise that I consider taking a job that emphasized my strengths and worked with my weaknesses. So I updated my resume this weekend, and I'm submitting it today."

Kate applied for the job, completed two interviews, and was hired. Now she has a position that is a better fit for her. She has a job that lets her do what she does best every day. She didn't try to force herself to get better at a job she didn't like. Instead, she looked for, and found, a better fit for her unique characteristics at the same company.

5. *If you can't find the right fit at your current employer, then quit and find a new full-time job.*

Identify the kinds of activities that put the spotlight on your strengths and make your weaknesses invisible or irrelevant. Look for jobs that include those activities, and start applying. Obviously, this isn't easy, but the results will make the process worthwhile.

I found a great illustration of this strategy in an advertisement for Fleet Feet Sports, a running apparel retail chain.

"MARTA IS SLOW. She used to be a barista. A really slow barista. She wanted the coffee to be really good, her boss wanted it to be really fast. He fired her. We hired her. Now she takes her time finding the right shoes for our customers. They don't mind the wait. You can't hurry fit."

Marta had an apparent weakness. She was slow. But her slowness wasn't a weakness; it was just a bad fit for her situation. It wasn't the right fit for a job as a barista.

Marta didn't need to become faster. She didn't need to hurry up. She needed to get out. She needed to find a job that valued her unique style, one that valued patience and attention to detail.

Marta found that job at Fleet Feet Sports. They didn't want her to change. They didn't want her to fix her weakness. In fact, they didn't see it as a weakness at all. They saw it as an essential qualification for the job.

If you are struggling in your current job or if you are on the verge of being fired, then you might need to change your job instead of trying to change yourself. If you are fast, impatient, hurried, anxious, or frenzied, find a job that values speed. If you are slow, lazy, unmotivated, particular, perfectionistic, detail oriented, or analytical, find a job that values accuracy, quality, and patience. You'll be happier. Your former employer will be happier. Your new employer will be happier. What could be better?

Although many people have found jobs that allow them to flaunt their weaknesses, it is easy to conclude that there is no career that fits your unique flaws. But sometimes the perfect job for you is hiding inside the very words that you use to describe your shortcomings.

YOU HAVE TO BE CONCEITED TO BE A STAR.

—Simon Cowell, *American Idol*

Maybe you are a control freak. I found a great blog post at Business-Pundit.com offering ten jobs for control freaks. If you are a control freak, don't despair—just seek out one of these career opportunities:

1. Air traffic controller—"If they're not a control freak, people may die."

2. Military officer

3. Chef

4. Surgeon—This is another example of how being a control freak can save lives.

5. Business consultant

6. Pilot

7. Professional organizer—"A priceless manifestation of control-freakish tendencies."

8. CEO

9. Accountant—That's why the job title is "controller."

10. Architect

Maybe we should add *movie director* to the list. Joseph McGinty Nichol ("McG") was the director for *Terminator Salvation, Charlie's Angels*, and a variety of television and Internet hits. In a recent Fast Company article, he admitted to being a control freak. I love the interviewer's response to McG's confession. "As afflictions go, it would be hard to find one better suited for a media mogul—or any mogul for that matter—than a seemingly endless capacity for control. To call McG a control freak might be uncharitable. Let's just say he's extremely attentive to detail."

The interviewer goes on to describe the frenzy of activity and decision overload that characterizes a movie set. This situation might overwhelm other people, but since McG is a control freak, this world is his "paradise." In other words, McG is a phenomenally successful and wealthy media mogul because of his weakness, not in spite of it. He has accomplished this success by finding the perfect fit for his particular problem—a situation in which his apparent weakness is a powerful strength.

Maybe you're too critical. There are many jobs for that, including food critic, music critic, and movie critic. You could also look into becoming a judge.

Simon Cowell, the notorious judge on *American Idol*, is a big jerk. He is mean and unfair. He is critical and harsh. He is conceited and cruel. He makes fun of contestants' height, weight, attractiveness, clothing, and singing ability (or lack thereof). He is also fantastically successful. He makes more money for himself and his employer, Sony, than any other person in a similar position.

Cowell is good—very good, maybe the best—at finding talented singers and helping them succeed in the music industry.

He knows good singing (and bad singing) when he hears it. Despite the millions of people who despise him, Cowell believes that he is honest and direct, not mean and nasty. He believes that he is actually doing people a favor when he confronts them with their lack of talent. He is trying to help them see the light and come to terms with their lack of ability so that they can move on with their lives.

In fact, Cowell is critical of the parents, music teachers, and friends who have failed to offer an honest assessment of many contestants' singing. Each of his strengths corresponds with one of his weaknesses. Is he honest or mean? Is he direct or harsh? Is he confident or conceited? He is all of these things, and they are inseparable. Furthermore, whether you like him or not, he has found the perfect fit for his critical nature. They call it judging for a reason.

If you're too analytical, become an analyst. *Wikipedia* lists more than fifteen different types of analysts in a variety of fields and defines an analyst as an individual whose "primary function is a deep examination of a specific, limited area."

THE WHOLE SECRET OF A SUCCESSFUL LIFE IS TO FIND OUT WHAT IT IS ONE'S DESTINY TO DO, AND THEN DO IT.

—Henry Ford

Even when the job title isn't in the words themselves, your flaws still hold the clues to your ideal workplace.

If you're a neat freak, become a professional organizer. You'd probably be surprised by the number of specialties in this area, including closet organizers, feng shui, ergonomics, and space planning. You can get started by joining the National Association of Professional Organizers.

6. Quit your full-time job, get a part-time job, and start a new business.

Some people aren't cut out to be employees. If your freak factor requires you to do your own thing but you are also somewhat risk-averse, this strategy can give you a greater sense of security and a modest source of income while you get your business off the ground. You could also get a new full-time job that is more flexible or has less responsibility and will allow you more time and/or energy to focus on your new business. My former job as a college professor gave me a tremendous amount of freedom to pursue my business as a speaker, trainer, and author. I quit that job in 2013 to run my speaking business full-time.

As a manager, I always struggled with the details. I had no shortage of ideas and goals for the future, but I didn't always follow them up with specific implementation plans. Because of this, my bosses regularly encouraged me to spend more time focusing on operations and less time developing new programs. Despite their prodding, I could never seem to motivate myself to dig into the day-to-day management of the department. This seems like a clear weakness, and to some extent, it was, in that particular situation.

However, my inability to manage the details was offset by my abilities as a strategic thinker. For example, I designed a new program to provide employment services to two hundred people with disabilities and initiated a $2 million capital campaign and building project in my first year on the job. My abilities were highly valued by my bosses, but they still wanted me to balance my big-picture focus with an appreciation for operational issues. They appreciated my strength but didn't see its connection to my weakness. At some point, I realized that the job just wasn't a good fit for my particular style.

I left management to become a professor and a consultant. I taught business strategy and helped my clients with strategic planning. In those roles, no one criticized me for failing to handle the details, because they hired me to help them see the big picture. My new environment highlighted the positive aspects of my characteristics and minimized the negative aspects of those same characteristics. In order to be more successful, you don't have to change yourself, you just need to change the situation.

7. Quit your job and start a business.

If your weaknesses include impulsiveness, overconfidence, or idealism, then this is the option for you. If you have no fear and just want to make the leap right now, then go for it. I strongly believe that the best way to find the right fit is to create it. Employers will never care as much about your future as you will, and they won't be able to creatively adapt to your unique characteristics as well as you can.

Jonathan Fields's book *Career Renegade* has some very practical and exciting examples of how people have turned their passions into viable businesses. For example, one husband and father turned his love of video games into a thriving business by writing books of tips and tricks for conquering new games.

Fields rejects the belief that jobs are the safe choice and entrepreneurship is risky. "As long as you're working for someone else, you'll never have the control you want." Additionally, your employer has priorities that can often conflict with your needs. "What's best for you is not their driving motivation."

Since the beginning of time, most people have been self-employed. They lived as farmers and hunters and had great freedom in deciding how and when to do their work. Organizations, managers, and employees, in contrast, are a relatively new phenomenon. When factory jobs were first introduced in England, most people referred to them as "wage slavery." I believe that people aren't designed to be employees and that working for others usually diminishes your happiness, fulfillment, and financial success.

Additionally, current trends in society and technology are making it more feasible to become a successful entrepreneur. Jonathan Fields challenges us to consider "what might unfold if you identified what you loved to do first, then tapped the wealth of tools, strategies and technologies that have only come onto the scene in the last few years to build a substantial living around what makes your entire life smile?"

Scott Adams was unhappy with his corporate job, so he quit. His Dilbert cartoons, which offer a scathing critique of most companies and their managers, have become some of the most popular comic strips in the country. He would never have had this same level of success as a cubicle dweller.

If you're considering entrepreneurship, the following questions might be helpful:

→ What specialized knowledge and skills do you already possess?

→ How could those skills be translated into a business?

→ Why does your current company employ you?

→ What valuable service do you provide?

→ How could you provide that same service to your company and/or other companies as a free agent?

→ Are there examples of other people who have already done this in your industry?

Another great way to discover potential career or business opportunities is to take a look at your hobbies.

→ What do you enjoy doing, even though you don't get paid for it?

→ What do you do voluntarily?

→ How do you spend your weekends?

→ How do you want to spend your retirement?

I'm not that good at delayed gratification. I don't want to wait until after work to do what I love. I want to enjoy what I do every day. I want to do what I do best every day and get paid for it.

Despite the many benefits of doing your own thing, Jun Loayza, cofounder of Untemplater.com, cautions that entrepreneurship isn't for everyone:

> The worst possible reason to become an entrepreneur is because you hate the corporate world. If you don't like your corporate job, it does not automatically follow that you will like starting your own company. It may just mean that you're in the wrong industry, the wrong company or that you chose the wrong career path.
>
> Ask yourself, "what career path suits me best?" You're going to have to figure this out on your own through trial and error and self reflection. If you've been an accountant for a year and you hate accounting, what are you still doing there? You should be networking, training yourself, and doing everything possible to change career paths into something you actually like to do.

9. ENTREPRENEURSHIP

The next sections will explore how the freak factor applies to management and strategy. Those sections are certainly beneficial for entrepreneurs as well, but I wanted to create a section specifically focused on people who run their own companies.

A few years ago, I started speaking at Entrepreneurs' Organization events. It might seem like entrepreneurs have this all figured out: they've reached the pinnacle. They started their own businesses, so they're doing what they want to do, when they want to do it. They don't have to fit into an organization that someone else created or follow their boss's rules. Or do they?

If entrepreneurs have investors, then they have multiple bosses with control over what they do and how to do it. Even for self-funded entrepreneurs, there are endless numbers of family members, friends, employees, partners, peers, and business experts giving them advice about how to run their company effectively. It can be difficult to maintain your freak factor against this onslaught of people identifying weaknesses in you and your company and telling you how to fix them. As Chris Brogan says in *The Freaks Shall Inherit the Earth*, a book about entrepreneurs, "freaks have to buck a lot of family and friends to go where their heart says to go."

As an entrepreneur, you also probably put pressure on yourself to get better and to adapt to changes in your business and industry. You might feel like you need to be more professional, more consistent, more visionary, calmer, or more enthusiastic. But you don't. You just need to be yourself.

As Cameron Herold, former COO of 1-800-GOT-JUNK? and author of *Double Double*, explains, "entrepreneurs are different. We're wired differently ... we're on the lunatic fringe ...

we're risk takers." Only 13 percent of Americans, just over one in ten, are entrepreneurs. Entrepreneurs are freaks, and that is a good thing. Brogan believes that "being different is what will keep you headed toward success." Don't deny it. Embrace it. Here's how.

Matt Curry is a serial entrepreneur and the founder of Curry's Auto Service. He has a lot of weaknesses, but he has one big weakness: attention deficit disorder (ADD). I want to use Curry's book, *The A.D.D. Entrepreneur*, to illustrate how the freak factor applies to entrepreneurs. I think Curry is a great example, because many entrepreneurs identify themselves as having ADD, and research shows some interesting links between ADD and entrepreneurship.

ONE OF THE QUICKEST, MOST RELIABLE WAYS TO DETERMINE THE BEST AND HIGHEST USE OF YOUR COMPANY'S HUMAN CAPITAL IS TO HAVE YOUR KEY EMPLOYEES TAKE PERSONALITY TESTS.

—Matt Curry, *The A.D.D. Entrepreneur*

Awareness

What are your strengths and weaknesses? Use all the feedback you've received and make a list. Gather all the assessments you've ever done and find the themes. Do the freak factor assessment with your partners, employees, friends, and family. Become clear on who you are, and make sure that others are clear as well. Curry believes that "we all have weaknesses. We all have flaws. I believe that for most of us, these defects or weaknesses—when channeled properly and perhaps even celebrated—can become our greatest strengths."

Acceptance

Now, don't try to fix any of the weaknesses. Acknowledge them. Accept them, but don't try to repair them.

As Curry says, "your flaw may actually be your superpower. I've never viewed ADD as a negative. Instead, I've embraced it." Herold agrees. "ADD doesn't have to be a problem at all. It's one of the key things that makes us successful as an entrepreneur … ADD allows us to see all the things related to our business that others miss … ADD is actually a strength."

Ask yourself this. What is the upside? What are the corresponding strengths? What is working? What isn't broken? That is what Curry does. "Focusing on my strengths helps put my 'weaknesses' into their proper place. My deficits don't define me and neither do yours … Make note of all the wonderful 'gifts' your disorder has given you."

Appreciation

Appreciation is about reframing our weaknesses as strengths. It's about finding the advantages hiding inside of our disadvantages. Curry argues that "when we pick negative words to describe our ADD, we cut ourselves down and diminish our abilities. But whenever we choose to put a positive spin on our condition, we lift ourselves up and come away empowered."

The founder of JetBlue Airways, David Neeleman, has said that if there was a pill that cured ADD, he wouldn't take it. Paul Orfalea, the billionaire founder of Kinko's, takes it one step further. He says that he thinks everyone should have dyslexia and ADD.

Edward Hallowell is the coauthor of *Driven to Distraction* and one of the leading experts on ADD. His research confirms a positive perspective on ADD. Hallowell created a table of "mirror traits" that describes both the weaknesses and the corresponding strengths of ADD. This is one more example of the connection between our flaws and our best traits.

Positive Trait	Negative Trait
Curious	Distractible
Creative	Impulsive
Energetic	Hyperactive, Restless
Eager	Intrusive
Sees Connections Others Miss	Can't Stay on Point
Totally Involved in What He/She Is Doing	Forgetful
Spontaneous	Disorganized
Persistent	Stubborn
Flashes of Brilliance	Inconsistent
Sensitive	Moody

Amplification

How could you exaggerate your unique qualities? What would happen if you did more of what people told you to stop doing?

Matt Curry says that he was "was obsessed ... with executing my vision. Being obsessive is usually a bad thing, but I used it in a positive way ... I've created numerous profitable companies, including the number one automotive repair chain ... and one of the fastest growing franchises in North America by making the most of my ADD ... That great stuff happened not despite my diagnosis, but because of it. I didn't conquer ADD. I leveraged it."

Do you start things but not finish them? Maybe you should start more things. People who do this are called serial entrepreneurs. They have a gift for getting things started, for creating, and for putting things in motion.

Are you impatient? Matt Curry is. "I don't like to wait in line and I hate to wait my turn. I'm restless, impatient, anxious, and seldom satisfied. I use these 'flaws' ... and aim them toward always trying to improve our product or service."

Robert Merrill, author of the Be Useful blog, isn't competitive or assertive. He doesn't like telling people what to do, he doesn't make a great first impression, and he doesn't handle stress well. Instead of trying to fix these weaknesses, he brags about them because they are clues to his strengths. For example, because he doesn't make a good first impression, he is "persistent in relationships and doesn't jump to conclusions."

Merrill includes this message for potential clients on his website: "If you invite me into the executive circle of your software-intensive business, you will probably find that I am different from most of you. That's precisely why I will be useful."

Don't try to minimize or moderate your freak factor. Brogan encourages entrepreneurs to look for "ways to allow your weirdness to be an asset, and not as the deficit that people have tried to convince you it is."

Alignment

Matt Curry argues that "you have to figure out what you and each member of your team excels in, and then put everybody on the task they're built for and let them do their thing … Details make me crazy … My best and highest use is in strategy and operations."

You have to do the same for yourself. You have to find or create the right fit for you. It is not the founder's job to do everything or to do the tasks that no one else wants to do. Just because you started the business doesn't mean that every task in that business is aligned with your unique characteristics. You need to identify the activities that match your strengths and focus more time and energy in those areas. Then, find people who are strong in the areas where you are weak and energized by those tasks you dislike (affiliation).

Avoidance

To be a more effective entrepreneur, you need to stop doing the activities that drain you and require you to overcome your weaknesses. Certainly, there are times when we all have to do things we don't like. But this isn't a sustainable strategy, because it uses valuable and limited self-control. As Chris Brogan reminds us, "Willpower is one of the smallest mental muscles you have."

We've been taught that endurance and perseverance are positive qualities. They are, but the best entrepreneurs know when to stop and when to quit. Brogan thinks that "we've got some strange ideas about quitting. We see it as a sign of weakness, of defeat, of failure. No way. Quitting is awesome. Quitting is the way to build strength and greatness. ... Sometimes, quitting is the coolest and most intelligent thing you can do."

We all have limited time, energy, and resources. Avoidance allows us to conserve those resources and use them in ways that maximize our effectiveness.

Affiliation

As the founder of a company, especially a small one, you might feel like you have to be good at everything. You don't. You can't. It's not possible. Don't try to do it all. Instead, find people who are strong where you are weak.

Cameron Herold argues that affiliation is vital for entrepreneurs, especially those with ADD. "Because we can't focus on stuff very well for a long period of time, we end up hiring others to do that for us ... starting things, getting a little bored, and passing it off to others. That's precisely what you need to do if you want to start and grow companies."

It can be difficult to implement this advice, because we think that it's not fair to give "bad jobs" to other people. But as Chris Brogan explains, "Plenty of not-so-creative people are still entrepreneurial enough to partner with ultracreative types, and they're more than happy to deal with the details that I and many other freaks might consider drudgeries."

Matt Curry's wife turned out to be the perfect business partner. Her strengths are an ideal complement to his. "When you have ADD, things fall through the cracks sometimes. But if you surround yourself with people whose superpowers fill in the gaps for you, that's when you strike gold. That's the way it's been for me with my wife, Judy … One of her superpowers is attention to detail, which is something I lack. Teaming up with Judy was the smartest thing I've ever done."

As we've already discussed, affiliation can be important in your personal life as well. As Chris Brogan admits, "I pay a really wonderful woman to wash, dry and fold my laundry."

It is also important to identify people who are different, just like you. We need people who complement us, but we also need people who affirm us. We need to belong. This can be difficult when only 10 percent of the population truly understands what it's like to be an entrepreneur.

Finding your people can also be a great opportunity to serve. Chris Brogan promises that "when you make it your business to find the people who are the same kind of freak as you, you'll profit from serving that community in some form." This explains the success of Entrepreneurs' Organization. It is a place where people can belong and where they can also serve.

10. MANAGEMENT

The freak factor framework can be used by managers and leaders to maximize employee engagement and productivity. It is a unique approach to two fundamental problems faced by most organizations.

PROBLEM #1: Employees are disengaged and unproductive.

Frustration, cynicism, and discontent are pervasive within today's companies. Research into employee motivation and performance consistently indicates that employees are not especially effective in their jobs and that many are looking for a way out

→ 72 percent of employees "dream of starting their own business" so they can do what they love and have more control over their life and work.[1]

→ Another study found that 67 percent of respondents "contemplate resigning from their job on a regular basis."[2]

→ A recent Gallup survey found that only 20 percent of employees feel like they have the opportunity to do what they do best every day. This means that 80 percent feel trapped by work that relies on them to excel in their areas of weakness.[3]

1 | David W. Moore, "Majority of American Want to Start Own Business," Gallup, April 12, 2005, http://www.gallup.com/poll/15832/majority-americans-want-start-own-business.aspx

2 | Rhonda Abrams, "Study: 72% of Workers Would Rather Work for Themselves," USA Today, last updated October 11, 2007, http://usatoday30.usatoday.com/money/smallbusiness/columnist/abrams/2007-10-11-workers-survey_N.htm

3 | Marcus Buckingham and Donald O. Clifton, "The Strengths Revolution," Gallup, January 22, 2001, http://www.gallup.com/businessjournal/547/strengths-revolution.aspx

Why is employee engagement so important? Engagement means the following:

- → Employees are involved and enthusiastic about their work.

- → Employees are willing and able to contribute to the company's success.

- → Employees are contributing discretionary time, energy, and thought.

What does it cost to have disengaged employees? Some research estimates that they cause approximately $250 billion in lost productivity each year. A 2003 study by ISR found that companies with disengaged employees saw their operating margins drop by 2 percent, while companies with engaged employees realized a 4 percent increase in margins.

What would it be worth to make your employees more engaged? Companies with engaged employees saw a 16 percent increase in share price, while the share price for companies with disengaged workers only increased 6 percent. Workers who are strongly engaged outperform their disengaged coworkers by 20-28 percent.

So how do we get employees to be more engaged? Unfortunately, the current way in which we answer this question just further hampers employee performance.

PROBLEM #2: Current strategies for improving performance actually make it worse.

We're trying to improve employee performance using the same methods that created the problem in the first place: rankings, evaluations, improvement plans, and required training. The implicit message of all these approaches is the same: there is something wrong with our employees, and we need to fix it.

Our perception that employees are broken and need to be fixed contributes to the problem of poor job performance. Our behavior toward our employees, which is based on these negative beliefs, further damages their performance. In other words, we think that our employees are broken, treat them like they are broken, and then wonder why they don't work.

Most people (59 percent in a Gallup study) think that fixing weaknesses will make them successful. However, we're putting huge amounts of effort into trying to get people to work on their faults, and it isn't helping. Marcus Buckingham and Richard Vosburgh argue that we cannot improve employee performance "through an endless quest to develop weaknesses."

The ineffectiveness of the conventional approach to improvement at work is illustrated by Nellie's experience during one of her performance evaluations. I met Nellie, founder of Arize Consulting, at a seminar for entrepreneurs. She shared the following story with me:

One incident in particular, midway through my career, stands out. Though the years have flown by, I still remember it as if it were yesterday.

I was in my manager's office going over my annual review. I was so excited. My 360-degree feedback was excellent. On a scale of 1 to 5, I was rated 4.7. As a senior project manager that was an awesome achievement. Project managers assign people more work to their already full plate along with a tight deadline and then chase them for a status updates [sic]. So, naturally, project managers are not the most popular people in the company.

My manager and I began walking through the annual review section by section. I was elated, that is until we got to the Interpersonal Skills section. I was in shock to see that I had only been given 3 out of 5. I believe that I am the ultimate people-person.

Without looking up at me, my manager tactfully went on to ask me to stop smiling and acting enthusiastic while I was at work. OUCH! My mind screamed "please pinch yourself and pray that you are having a nightmare." This could not be happening. Job descriptions frequently read "enthusiastic, results-oriented professional with ..."

My manager explained that he thought I was fantastic and his best, most productive and dependable employee. However, one of the senior executives was annoyed by my natural enthusiasm. My boss asked me to stop smiling at this executive when I passed her in the hallways. "You can acknowledge her. Just do not smile."

Wow! This pierced my being. I was born enthusiastic, smiling and looking at the brighter side of everything. His quote from her was "if people want sunshine they could go outside." The fact that I had delivered 180% of my set goals went by the wayside.

Nellie's story has a happy ending, but her eventual success was not facilitated by her manager or her organization. She succeeded because she refused to accept this ridiculous criticism and change her approach to work:

I have a love and passion for life and people. I knew immediately that I could not change this about me because it is deeply ingrained. Fast forward to today. I run a business and am a successful business consultant, change manager, and coach; all of which requires that a person be enthusiastic, encouraging, and genuinely caring. I am so glad that my enthusiasm was not easily turned off; otherwise this high-level executive, who I highly respected, would have killed the precise trait that propels me.

This manager was doing his best to improve Nellie's performance. He thought that, by pointing out her flaws and asking her to change, he would get the desired result. However, he almost inadvertently killed the traits that propelled her.

We Need a Different Approach

The seven steps in the freak factor framework focus on identifying and maximizing employees' strengths instead of trying to fix their weaknesses. As Peter Drucker, the father of modern management, explains, "organizations exist to make employees' strengths effective and their weaknesses irrelevant."

"FIND THE FREAKS! SIGN 'EM UP! MAKE 'EM YOUR PARTNERS! LET 'EM HELP YOU MAKE A REVOLUTION!"

—Tom Peters

Awareness

Weaknesses are important clues to employees' strengths. As such, we need to start by identifying employees' strengths and weaknesses before they even begin working for us. This is also important for our existing employees. We should assess our teams, work groups, departments, and divisions in order to understand our people better and help them understand each other. Awareness is the foundation for all other aspects of the freak factor framework. Until we know our employees' strengths and weaknesses, we can't move forward.

Publix Super Markets has been on *Fortune's* list of "The Best Companies to Work for in America" for twenty-five years. Publix believes that it is possible to measure a job candidate's natural tendency to provide great service. Its hiring decisions are based on a person's strengths and their fit with the company's culture.

Acceptance

Apparent weaknesses are strengths in disguise. Effective management is not about changing people; it is about accepting and respecting who they are and finding ways to help them succeed.

Best Buy manages employees with a strengths-based philosophy, and its managers "leverage employee strengths in their jobs rather than focusing on improving weaknesses." Best Buy's revolutionary Results Only Work Environment (ROWE) provides an unprecedented level of autonomy and allows employees to work in ways that match their strengths and minimize their weaknesses. "Each person is free to do whatever they want, whenever they want as long as the work gets done." This approach has led to a 41 percent increase in productivity and a 90 percent decrease in turnover.

Saddleback Church, located in Lake Forest, California, is the eighth-largest church in America. The church's senior pastor, Rick Warren, is the author of *The Purpose Driven Life*, which has sold more than twenty-five million copies. Warren believes that "the secret of achieving results is to focus on your strengths, and the strengths of those you work with, rather than focusing on weaknesses." He manages his organization and his employees and volunteers with this philosophy.

Warren argues that "great organizations position people for success rather than trying to eliminate all their weaknesses … When an employee fails because he doesn't have the strengths to match the job, the fault is management's, not the employee's … In order to use the strengths of people we must be willing to put up with their weaknesses."

Appreciation

People succeed because of their weaknesses, not in spite of them. As managers, we need to identify the unique value that each employee can contribute. This should be part of the evaluation process. Instead of trying to find and fix weaknesses, we can focus on the person's strengths and look for ways to deploy those strengths at work.

Ann Taylor, a women's clothing retailer, helps managers to understand that their employees' weaknesses are linked to their strengths. Because of this perspective, managers don't try to fix their employees' flaws. Instead, they find partners within the organization that complement the employees' weaknesses. Managers also attempt to adapt their own approaches to accommodate employees' unique styles.

For example, Claudia was very analytical and intense. She had a strong need to know as much information as possible about issues that affected her work. When she didn't get that information in a timely manner, she got frustrated, and this created tension between her and her manager. It also created problems within the entire work team.

An average manager might have identified this behavior as a weakness and lectured Claudia on how to control her need for information. Judi, however, realized that this "weakness" was an aspect of Claudia's greatest strength: her analytical mind. Claudia would never be able to rein it in, at least not for long.

Instead of trying to fix Claudia's weakness, her manager made an effort to dramatically increase the amount of information that she shared with Claudia. They scheduled regular meetings and daily phone calls. This allowed Claudia to focus more time and energy on her strengths, and it improved her performance.

Amplification

We need to encourage and develop each individual's unique abilities. Great managers help people to become more of who they are. One way to do this is to train strengths. Too often, our training efforts are focused on remediating weaknesses. A more effective approach is to help employees amplify their existing strengths through books, seminars, and coaching.

We also need to stop cross-training our employees and focus on specialization instead. People aren't machines, and their skills and interests are not necessarily interchangeable. Best Buy's employees are geeks that know a lot about a narrow range of products. A mobile phone expert won't necessarily be an expert in car stereo installation. How could you help your people learn even more about their current job responsibilities?

Patagonia hires "dirtbags." Instead of looking for employees with business skills or sales experience, Patagonia selects people who have a natural passion for the outdoors. This is something that cannot be taught in a training program. "Dirtbags" have many weaknesses, but these are less important than their strengths.

Like Publix Super Markets, W. L. Gore & Associates has also been on *Fortune's* list of "The Best Companies to Work for in America" for twenty-five years. Its employees do not have traditional job descriptions. They are allowed to add new responsibilities that match their strengths (alignment) and can decline those that don't (avoidance). Instead of following development plans developed by their supervisors, employees create their own customized personal growth plans.

Alignment

Instead of forcing people to fit in, we need to help them find the right fit. We need to help employees discover activities and responsibilities that match their unique characteristics.

Since people don't change that much, we need to get the right people in the first place. We need to identify the strength/weakness combinations that match the needs of our team and to clearly understand what trade-offs we are comfortable making. We won't have to adapt as much if we find people who fit the requirements of the job.

Unfortunately, most companies spend far more money on training people to fit in than they do on selecting people for a particular job. Once we find the right people for the job, we'll need to continually work with our employees to help them identify and create responsibilities that match their unique characteristics.

One way to maximize alignment is to let people choose their work. 3M and Google know this, and that is why they allow their employees to work on projects they are passionate about during the work week. Atlassian, an Australian software company, regularly allows all their employees to take twenty-four consecutive hours to develop their own innovative products or service ideas. Red Hat, *Wikipedia*, and the Apache Software Foundation run almost exclusively on the efforts of willing volunteers.

Lest this seem like some kind of touchy-feely employee-centric nonsense, another important action step is to fire faster. In the words of Marcus Buckingham, "Never stop caring for your people. You will rarely fire a person too early. Tough love is built on love." We waste far too much time trying to turn people into the person that we need. If an employee doesn't fit, we shouldn't try to make them fit. We should set them free.

SAS Institute assesses and categorizes clinical programmers based on their strengths and weaknesses. The four profiles are scientist, statistician, developer, and lead programmer. Managers are trained to assign tasks to programmers based on their strengths, instead of trying to fix their weaknesses. SAS believes that employees will be more motivated and perform at higher levels when they are allowed to focus on activities that fit their strengths and avoid those that rely on their weaknesses.

At SAS, managers are given scenarios with specific projects to be completed by certain people. They are then asked to choose the right person for each task. The managers are taught to consider what each person likes to do and does well along with what he or she doesn't like to do and does poorly: "Assigning projects might be the most critical aspect of allowing programmers to exercise their full motivation. Give a highly motivated programmer a job that he/she does not see as important or is not good at, and you will undoubtedly see his/her motivation decrease sharply."

SAS differentiates types of work, identifying which will be best assigned to each profile. Lead programmers are charged with project organization, scientists are charged with documenting the details of programming, developers spend most of their time actually developing, and statisticians focus on how the programming compares to statistical models. The whole idea is to let developers be developers and scientists be scientists without everyone needing to be everything.

Avoidance

If we want people to be the best, we need to let them be the worst. It isn't possible to be the best at everything. If we are helping employees to do more work that matches their strengths, then we also need to allow employees to stop doing work that puts a spotlight on their weaknesses.

Instead of trying to change people to fit particular positions, transfer them. Help them find the right match between who they are and what they do. This option is especially feasible in large corporations where there are a wide variety of positions.

Instead of rehabilitating a difficult employee, try redirecting him or her instead. It can be easier to change a job than to change a person. It is often possible to make a slight change in job responsibilities (alignment) and see a large improvement in performance. As Jim Collins suggests in *Good to Great*, it isn't enough to simply get the right people in the right seats. We sometimes need to redesign the seats and change the seating arrangement on the bus.

Could we assign employees more of the work that they do well? Can we eliminate aspects of the work that they do poorly? Think of this like pruning a tree. Eliminating the unproductive aspects of people's jobs can give them more time and energy to invest in the areas in which they are productive.

Stryker Corporation, a large surgical equipment company, has documented significant financial gains from allowing employees to avoid activities that draw on their weaknesses. In one example, Stryker saved over $1 million by moving an employee from a role as an individual performer—where he struggled—into a supervisory position—where he thrived. His new role also changed his level of engagement at work. His supervisors felt that his attitude and performance had critically improved.

Another employee struggled with paperwork but excelled in sales. The employee's performance improved significantly once he was no longer required to complete paperwork. His managers at Stryker eliminated the problem by redistributing the paperwork among team members who could more comfortably balance it with their engineering contributions.

Affiliation

Effective managers create teams with complementary strengths and weaknesses. Although no single employee is going to be perfectly balanced and well-rounded, we need to build work groups and departments that include employees whose strengths and weaknesses complement those of their coworkers.

Managers are too busy trying to make everyone the same. We use cross-training and other methods to make everyone capable of doing any job at any time, or we assemble homogenous teams of people with the same strengths and the same weaknesses.

Very few employees are completely effective on their own, but they can be a valuable part of the team. We need to find team members with complementary skills and help them work together to accomplish the tasks that need to be done. By combining people instead of fixing them, we can improve the performance of each individual and of the entire team. Teamwork doesn't mean that everybody does the same thing; it means that everyone contributes what they do best.

I met Kelly when she was an undergraduate student in my management class. She was a great salesperson. Selling seemed like the ideal fit for her skills and personality. She was a natural.

Kelly was so good at her job that she sold insurance to me during the class. She didn't wait for a break. When I was complaining about the lack of service from my current insurance agent, she raised her hand and suggested that I switch to her agency. I filled out the forms the next week and was a customer before the course was over.

Kelly sounds like the perfect employee, but she had a problem. She was incredibly disorganized and was inefficient with the essential administrative tasks that her job required. She frequently lost important forms, which created major inconveniences for her clients and caused costly delays within her agency. Her office was littered with piles of papers, discarded fast-food containers, dirty dishes, and boxes overflowing with marketing materials. This is a classic problem with salespeople. She was terrible at paperwork but wonderful with people work.

Kelly's manager realized that Kelly's talent for sales was a rare and valuable gift. Instead of criticizing Kelly for poor performance or sending her to training, Kelly's boss simply hired another person to handle the paperwork and create an organized work environment for Kelly. This freed Kelly to do more of what she did so well and made her much happier and more fulfilled in her work. In return, Kelly's boss got increased sales and revenue.

Application

As managers, we are also employees. The principles in *The Freak Factor* apply to us as well. It isn't enough to help our employees to flaunt their weaknesses. As managers, we have to become freaks as well.

We fail when we try to please everyone by becoming perfect, by fixing all our weaknesses. We fail when we believe that it is possible for everyone to like us, respect us, and appreciate us.

Our employees are all too aware of our apparent weaknesses and wish that we could overcome them to become more effective managers. It can be tempting to try to become a perfect, well-rounded leader, but this is not an effective strategy. Instead, we should acknowledge that we cannot please everyone, hire employees who are strong where we are weak, look for activities that fit our unique styles, and admit our flaws to our employees.

When assessing potential job candidates, it is important to consider more than just the job responsibilities. We should also consider candidates' fit with our management styles. For example, if we want employees who take initiative, then we shouldn't hire folks who require a lot of direction.

We should also seek out people who complement specific weaknesses that we have. Additionally, we need mentors and organizational allies who will help us create an environment that highlights our strengths and minimizes our weaknesses.

We can't please everyone, but we can help them understand and accept our apparent weaknesses. It's important to be honest with our employees, managers, and coworkers about our strengths and weaknesses. This will help foster honesty about their strengths and weaknesses as well.

One way to foster this honesty is to write a "how to deal with me" memo. Marshall Goldsmith suggests this approach in his book *What Got You Here Won't Get You There*. Even though Goldsmith's job is to help successful executives overcome their interpersonal quirks to become even more effective, he admits that this isn't always possible. Because of this reality, Goldsmith encourages his clients to write a memo to their employees that outlines their unique qualities and explains how to effectively deal with their personal and managerial idiosyncrasies. This advice is supported by persuasion research, which indicates that admitting weaknesses makes our ideas more powerful.

George is a great example of affiliation. He is a manager at a small magazine publisher who doesn't like to accompany his clients, mainly vendors and advertisers, to the endless formal events in his industry. He finds many of the people boring and has a difficult time engaging them in conversation, so he doesn't go (avoidance). He told his employees that these banquets drain him of his energy and that he doesn't perform well in those situations.

In contrast, Brad, one of George's employees, truly enjoys getting dressed up and interacting with advertising clients at formal gatherings. Because of this, George now delegates these activities to Brad (alignment, affiliation). This allows George to focus on other areas in which he is more interested and more skilled, and it allows Brad to grow in his career and to build relationships with key players in the publishing industry.

FAMOUS FREAK: Paul Orfalea

Paul grew up in a hardworking, middle-class family in Southern California. In second grade, he still didn't know the alphabet. Efforts by his teachers, parents, and siblings didn't seem to help. He was eventually diagnosed with both dyslexia and ADHD (awareness). After failing a few grades and being expelled from several schools, Orfalea finally graduated from high school with a 1.2 grade point average and a ranking of 1,482nd out of 1,500 students.

Based on his disability and poor performance in school, most people wouldn't have predicted success for Paul. In fact, Paul himself was often concerned that he would end up homeless. He started a small business selling school supplies and copies from a store so small that he had to move the copier out to the sidewalk. The business eventually grew to twelve hundred locations in ten different countries, and in 2004, Paul Orfalea sold Kinko's to FedEx for more than $2 billion.

How did a dyslexic guy who can't read or write build such a successful business? Orfalea argues that he succeeded because of his disability, not in spite of it (appreciation). Because of his weaknesses, he had to trust others and rely on them to help him run the business. For example, he needed people to assist him with correspondence. This evolved into a culture of teamwork and collaboration that separated Kinko's from its competitors. Paul hired people who were strong where he was weak (affiliation).

Because Orfalea was restless, he spent most of his time out of his office and in the stores, observing the practices of frontline employees. Because he was impulsive, he quickly implemented new ideas throughout the organization. His intuitive intelligence and racing mind made him impatient and easily frustrated, but many employees credit these traits with creating a sense of urgency that motivated people to make changes and improvements (amplification).

Orfalea wrote *Copy This! Lessons from a Hyperactive Dyslexic Who Turned a Bright Idea into One of America's Best Companies* with journalist Ann Marsh, but because of his dyslexia, he's never been able to read his own book. In it, he credits his disabilities for his success and says that he thinks everyone should have dyslexia and ADHD. During his many speaking engagements, he advises audiences to "like yourself, not despite your flaws and so-called deficits, but because of them."

Paul Orfalea didn't just appreciate his own weaknesses; he also created an organization that appreciated the weaknesses of its employees. He turned Kinko's into a freak factory by demonstrating sensitivity for the limitations of others, such as stubbornness, impatience, disorganization, and impulsiveness. Since he wasn't perfect, he didn't expect perfection from others (acceptance). He readily admitted his own flaws and accepted the flaws of his employees. Because he couldn't do everything well and relied on others to complete essential tasks, he also allowed others to find team members who complemented their weaknesses.

Additionally, Orfalea wasn't afraid to be different, and he encouraged his employees to approach their work in unique and creative ways (amplification). This created a culture of innovation, trust, and teamwork that made Kinko's a perennial favorite on the *Fortune* 100 Best Companies to Work For list.

How can you begin to follow in Orfalea's footsteps and create your own freak factory?

Implementation

The best way to implement these strategies in your organization is to hire me to help you coordinate the process. However, I want to provide you with an outline for how to create a freak factory on your own.

Phase 1—Educate Leaders

➜ **Increase the self-awareness of the team/department supervisors and managers through assessment.**

1. Strengths

2. Weaknesses

3. Strength/weakness combinations

➜ **Explore freak factor strategies with group training.**

1. Increase awareness of employee weaknesses.

2. Reframe weaknesses as strengths.

3. Create alignment between employees' strengths and their job responsibilities.

   a. Redefine jobs to create a better fit.

   b. Transfer employees to areas that match their unique strengths.

      c.   Promote real teamwork by identifying employees with complementary characteristics.

    4.   Fire the wrong people. If revised job responsibilities or transfers cannot provide an employee with the right fit, he or she may need to find alignment at a different organization.

    5.   Write a "how to deal with me" memo. Managers need to understand their unique strengths and weaknesses and communicate them to their employees. No employee is perfect, and the same is true for managers.

➜ **Develop action plans.**

    1.   Personal development: Managers need to have a plan for improvement based on maximizing their strengths, not fixing their weaknesses.

    2.   Employee development: Managers need to create employee improvement plans based on maximizing employees' strengths, not fixing their weaknesses.

Phase 2—Educate Staff

➜ **Provide freak factor training for employees (this can happen simultaneously with Phase 1).**

➜ **Improve each employee's self-awareness through assessment.**

    1.   Strengths

2. Weaknesses

3. Strength/weakness combinations

➜ **Help employees reframe their weaknesses (and those of their coworkers and managers) by facilitating a discussion of each team member's unique characteristics.**

➜ **Get employees' feedback regarding alignment, amplification, and avoidance.**

1. Whose job responsibilities match their strengths?

2. Whose job responsibilities call on their weaknesses?

3. When are they the most engaged and productive?

4. When are they disengaged and unproductive?

➜ **Foster greater teamwork.**

1. Identify employees with complementary skills and abilities.

2. Create partnerships based on complementary strengths and weaknesses.

3. Adjust individual work responsibilities within the team.

Phase 3—Implement and Refine

➜ **Make departmental changes based on the information gathered in Phases 1 and 2.**

→ **Evaluate results and adjust accordingly.**

1. Perform pre-tests and post-tests of employee engagement and/or productivity.

2. Interview managers and employees.

3. Adjust existing organizational measurements and standards.

→ **Continually communicate with managers regarding challenges and successes.**

→ **Begin the process in other departments and in senior management.**

Phase 4—Organizational Changes

→ **Create strengths-based job profiles identifying the ideal characteristics for particular roles.**

→ **Create strengths-based performance evaluation processes.**

→ **Create career tracks and compensation systems that reward engagement and productivity.**

→ **Train managers and employees to facilitate freak factor training and assessment.**

11. STRATEGY

In her book, *Different*, Harvard marketing professor Youngme Moon argues that "the ability to compete is dependent on the ability to differentiate from competitors." However, she goes on to say that "the number of companies who are truly able to achieve competitive separation is depressingly small." This is because companies tend to define their strengths and weaknesses using the same measurements and standards as their competitors. This leads to homogeneity, not differentiation. When everyone is trying to build on the same strengths and eliminate the same weaknesses, all companies start to look the same. So how can you create one of the few organizations that becomes extraordinary? How can you succeed where most organizations fail? It starts with a new perspective on organizational strengths and weaknesses.

Awareness

Almost every strategic planning process begins with an analysis of an organization's strengths, weaknesses, opportunities, and threats (SWOT). I've designed an organizational version of the freak factor assessment to help you see your organization's strengths and weaknesses in a new light.

Identifying Your Strengths

1. Put check marks in the boxes to the left of the positive characteristics of your organization, people, culture, and/or products and services.

2. If you notice any characteristics that are definitely not strengths of your organization, draw a line through them.

3. Choose your organization's top five strengths, and rank them from one to five (one being the strongest).

X	Strengths	Rank
	1. Large, Substantial	
	2. Responsive, Quick	
	3. Local, Familiar	
	4. Global, Exotic	
	5. Inexpensive	
	6. Luxurious	
	7. Activist, Revolutionary	
	8. Conventional, Traditional	
	9. Handcrafted, Unique	
	10. Standardized, Uniform	
	11. Simple, Clean	
	12. Intricate, Elaborate	
	13. Automated, Programmed	
	14. Personal, Individualized	
	15. Disposable	
	16. Permanent, Lasting	

x	Strengths	Rank
	17. Objective, Rational	
	18. Sensitive, Caring	
	19. Fun, Entertaining	
	20. Serious, Professional	
	21. Patient, Deliberate	
	22. Spontaneous, Instinctive	
	23. Reliable, Dependable	
	24. Exciting, High Performance	
	25. Fast Growth	
	26. Steady, Consistent Growth	
	27. New, Innovative	
	28. Reputable, Established	
	29. Cooperative, Friendly	
	30. Competitive, Assertive	
	31. Vigilant, Alert	
	32. Satisfied, Content	
	33. Systematic, Deliberate	
	34. Agile, Responsive	
	35. Focused, Specialized	
	36. Diversified	
	37. Lavish, Extravagant	
	38. Frugal, Thrifty	
	39. Cautious, Careful	
	40. Courageous, Audacious	
	41. Challenging, Stimulating	
	42. Agreeable, Conciliatory	
	43. Daring, Bold	
	44. Refined, Conservative	

Identifying Your Weaknesses

1. Put check marks in the boxes to the left of
    negative characteristics of your organization,
    people, culture, and/or products and services.

2. If you notice any characteristics that
    are definitely not weaknesses of your
    organization, draw a line through them.

3. Choose your organization's top five
    weaknesses and rank them from one
    to five (one being the weakest).

x	Weaknesses	Rank
	1. Bulky, Cumbersome	
	2. Small, Weak	
	3. Regular, Ordinary	
	4. Foreign, Unfamiliar	
	5. Cheap, Low Quality	
	6. Expensive, Overpriced	
	7. Rebellious, Radical	
	8. Old-Fashioned, Conforming	
	9. Irregular, Rough	
	10. Ordinary, Common	
	11. Plain, Dull	
	12. Complex	
	13. Impersonal, Cold	
	14. Labor-Intensive, Unpredictable	
	15. Poor Quality, Shoddy	
	16. Fixed, Unchanging	

x	Weaknesses	Rank
	17. Detached, Insensitive	
	18. Vulnerable, Emotional	
	19. Silly, Immature	
	20. Somber, Humorless	
	21. Slow, Indecisive	
	22. Impatient, Impulsive	
	23. Boring, Predictable	
	24. Unreliable, Inconsistent	
	25. Unstable, Volatile	
	26. Slow, Plodding	
	27. Untested, Unproven	
	28. Old, Outdated	
	29. Passive, Reactive	
	30. Aggressive, Hostile	
	31. Anxious, Fearful	
	32. Complacent, Ignorant	
	33. Bureaucratic, Inflexible	
	34. Reactive, Unpredictable	
	35. Limited, Restricted, Narrow	
	36. Unfocused, Scattered	
	37. Wasteful, Reckless	
	38. Stingy, Cheap	
	39. Fearful, Timid	
	40. Careless, Foolish	
	41. Confrontational, Demanding	
	42. Weak, Submissive	
	43. Irreverent, Offensive	
	44. Boring, Uninspiring	

Acceptance

Once you know your company's strengths and weaknesses, what should you do? The conventional wisdom is to build on strengths and fix weaknesses. As you already know, I disagree with this approach, because every weakness has a corresponding strength. So let's look at the connections between your organization's strengths and weaknesses.

x	Strengths	Weaknesses	x
	1. Large, Substantial	1. Bulky, Cumbersome	
	2. Responsive, Quick	2. Small, Weak	
	3. Local, Familiar	3. Regular, Ordinary	
	4. Global, Exotic	4. Foreign, Unfamiliar	
	5. Inexpensive	5. Cheap, Low Quality	
	6. Luxurious	6. Expensive, Overpriced	
	7. Activist, Revolutionary	7. Rebellious, Radical	
	8. Conventional, Traditional	8. Old-Fashioned, Conforming	
	9. Handcrafted, Unique	9. Irregular, Rough	
	10. Standardized, Uniform	10. Ordinary, Common	
	11. Simple, Clean	11. Plain, Dull	
	12. Intricate, Elaborate	12. Complex	
	13. Automated, Programmed	13. Impersonal, Cold	
	14. Personal, Individualized	14. Labor-Intensive, Unpredictable	
	15. Disposable	15. Poor Quality, Shoddy	
	16. Permanent, Lasting	16. Fixed, Unchanging	
	17. Objective, Rational	17. Detached, Insensitive	
	18. Sensitive, Caring	18. Vulnerable, Emotional	

x	Strengths	Weaknesses	x
	19. Fun, Entertaining	19. Silly, Immature	
	20. Serious, Professional	20. Somber, Humorless	
	21. Patient, Deliberate	21. Slow, Indecisive	
	22. Spontaneous, Instinctive	22. Impatient, Impulsive	
	23. Reliable, Dependable	23. Boring, Predictable	
	24. Exciting, High Performance	24. Unreliable, Inconsistent	
	25. Fast Growth	25. Unstable, Volatile	
	26. Steady, Consistent Growth	26. Slow, Plodding	
	27. New, Innovative	27. Untested, Unproven	
	28. Reputable, Established	28. Old, Outdated	
	29. Cooperative, Friendly	29. Passive, Reactive	
	30. Competitive, Assertive	30. Aggressive, Hostile	
	31. Vigilant, Alert	31. Anxious, Fearful	
	32. Satisfied, Content	32. Complacent, Ignorant	
	33. Systematic, Deliberate	33. Bureaucratic, Inflexible	
	34. Agile, Responsive	34. Reactive, Unpredictable	
	35. Focused, Specialized	35. Limited, Restricted, Narrow	
	36. Diversified	36. Unfocused, Scattered	
	37. Lavish, Extravagant	37. Wasteful, Reckless	
	38. Frugal, Thrifty	38. Stingy, Cheap	
	39. Cautious, Careful	39. Fearful, Timid	
	40. Courageous, Audacious	40. Careless, Foolish	
	41. Challenging, Stimulating	41. Confrontational, Demanding	
	42. Agreeable, Conciliatory	42. Weak, Submissive	
	43. Daring, Bold	43. Irreverent, Offensive	
	44. Refined, Conservative	44. Boring, Uninspiring	

The opposite of acceptance is rejection. Even if we are able to accept our company's unique strengths and weaknesses, we will certainly face both resistance and rejection. As Alex Bogusky warns, "Life conspires to beat the rebel out of you."

It simply isn't possible to find an approach that makes all customers happy. Anything we do will end up alienating someone. If we believe that our company can please everyone by becoming perfect, by fixing all of our weaknesses, then we will fail. Not everyone likes Starbucks, McDonald's, Apple, or Walmart, and yet they are very successful companies.

Our companies' products or services can't make everyone happy, and it is futile to try. Frances Frei and Anne Morriss encourage managers to "decide what trade-offs you will make— where you will do things badly, even very badly, in the service of great." Success is about delighting the right customers and being willing to make other customers unhappy.

Celebrity chef Rachel Ray doesn't mind being criticized: "If you spend so much time thinking about the people who dislike what it is you're doing, you're doing a disservice to the people that employ you. I'm not employed by those people. I work for the people that want the type of food I write [about], the type of food we share with people."[1]

One way to deal more effectively with rejection is to reframe it as a sign that you are doing something right. In her book *Fascinate*, Sally Hogshead argues that "if you're not eliciting a negative response from someone, then you're probably not very compelling to anyone." Being rejected by at least some potential customers means that you are on the right track.

---

1 | Rene Lynch, "Ha Ha Haters—Rachel Ray Is Laughing All the Way to the Bank," Los Angeles Times, March 7, 2009, http://latimesblogs.latimes.com/dailydish/2009/03/ha-ha-haters--.html

Appreciation

When it comes to competition, it is tempting to compare our organizations to others that seem more successful or more popular. We imagine that they have big strengths and no weaknesses, but this isn't true. As we've already discussed, our organizations' apparent weaknesses are also strengths, and the competition's obvious strengths are also weaknesses. We need to find ways to capitalize on our organizations' unique characteristics and to use our apparent weaknesses to our advantage.

In *Enemy of the State*, a conspiracy-theory thriller, Gene Hackman tries to help Will Smith evade the government agents who are trying to capture him. Smith sees his situation as hopeless, but Hackman changes his perspective by offering a lesson in guerrilla warfare: "You use your weakness as strength. They're big and you're small. But that means they're slow and you're fast. They're exposed and you're hidden." He reframes apparent strengths (being big) as weaknesses (slow and exposed) and apparent weaknesses (being small) as strengths (fast and hidden).

A great example of appreciation can be found in the discount retail industry. Walmart's main strength is low prices, but its weaknesses include poor-quality merchandise, long lines, and unhelpful employees. Meanwhile, Target's main strengths are higher-quality products from well-known designers, attractive stores, and helpful associates who are quick to open a new checkout lane. Target's weakness is that its prices are not as low as those at Walmart.

What would happen if, instead of appreciating them, Walmart tried to fix its weaknesses? What would happen to its low prices—its primary strength—as it added better products and extra employees at the registers? The answer is simple. Walmart's prices would climb, thus diminishing its strength.

What if Target decided to fix its weakness by lowering prices? What would happen to the level of customer service and the great products—which give Target its advantage—if it focused more on cutting costs? Again, the answer is straightforward. Target's quality and service would decrease, thus diminishing its strength.

For proof of this, just look at Kmart. It provides an illustration of what happens when a company or individual loses focus and tries to fix weaknesses instead of focusing on strengths. Kmart's historical leadership in discount retail was based on the Blue Light Special, a symbol of low prices. However, Kmart did not focus exclusively on this price advantage and began to lose customers to Walmart.

Kmart then began adding designer products from celebrities like Martha Stewart, but it wasn't quite ready to shed its low-price image. This allowed Target to capture higher-income customers who were design-conscious, while Walmart attracted lower-income customers who were cost-conscious.

Kmart's efforts to fix its weaknesses ultimately led to bankruptcy. Kmart became undifferentiated. It wasn't the best at anything, so customers had no reason to shop at its stores. Kmart's failure illustrates the dangers of trying to eliminate weaknesses and be more well-rounded. As Harvard marketing professor Youngme Moon explains in her book, *Different*, "True differentiation is rarely a function of well-roundedness; it is typically a function of lopsidedness."

There is a compelling reason to go to Walmart: low prices. There are compelling reasons to go to Target: better service and design. But there is no compelling reason to go to Kmart: its prices aren't the lowest, and its service and design aren't the best. Kmart is just mediocre in both areas, so people don't shop there.

IT'S SO EASY TO TRY TO COMPROMISE, TO DO BOTH, TO FIT IN AND STAND OUT. THERE LIES FAILURE.

—Seth Godin, *Linchpin*

What is true for individuals is also true for companies. When we try to fix our weaknesses, we end up damaging the corresponding strengths. Our efforts to make our companies better can end up making them worse. As Frances Frei and Anne Morriss explain in their book, *Uncommon Service*, "striving for all-around excellence leads directly to mediocrity."

If we really appreciated our companies' weaknesses, we would amplify them instead of trying to fix them. We would exaggerate our apparent flaws.

IF YOU CAN'T FIX IT, FEATURE IT.

—Gerald Weinberg, *The Secrets of Consulting*

Amplification

It might sound ridiculous to amplify your organization's weaknesses. In fact, this is exactly the opposite of what most companies (and politicians) do. The traditional approach involves highlighting positive features and repairing or obscuring any negative ones.

For example, a bag of Domino sugar explains that "sugar is a 100% natural simple carbohydrate. Carbohydrates are an important part of any balanced diet. Sugar contains no fat or cholesterol and has 15 calories per teaspoon." Domino makes it sound like the perfect food.

Domino's strategy seems to make sense. Why would you want to tell potential customers about what's wrong with your product? It seems ridiculous, and that is why very few companies do it.

However, there's a major problem with this approach. We all know that sugar isn't the perfect food, and that undermines our ability to trust Domino. The company isn't being honest. We know that nothing is perfect. Pretending that your product is flawless hurts your brand. In contrast, acknowledging that your product isn't perfect makes it easier to love your brand.

According to the Heath brothers, authors of *Made to Stick*, openly admitting limitations helps us build trust. This is true when discussing our own limitations or those of our ideas, products, or services: "We've all come across salespeople who are reluctant to admit any weakness in their product or service, no matter how insignificant. As many a sales guru has pointed out, building trust involves being candid, and being candid involves admitting that your products aren't flawless. Admitting weakness can, oddly enough, make your core ideas more powerful." Similarly, brand consultant Vicki Stirling believes that "admitting mistakes and flaws are actually really good tools to encourage loyalty."

And to be clear, this isn't about admitting and then apologizing for your product's weaknesses. Remember, *flaunt* means "to parade without shame." Weaknesses aren't something to be ashamed of; they are something to celebrate. So what would that look like in a business context?

Alex Bogusky and his ad agency, Crispin Porter + Bogusky, are the creators of many well-known and successful advertising campaigns. His successes include the resurrection of Burger King and the introduction of the Mini car to America. Both of these transformations were based on amplifying weaknesses, not minimizing them: "Instead of hiding qualities that may seem negative—such as Mini's tiny proportions or Burger King's fat content—Crispin exploits them. 'It's part of your job as a marketer to find the truths in a company, and you let them shine through in whatever weird way it might be.'"

For example, the slogan for Irv's Men's Store in Chicago is "Inconveniently located." Its radio commercials have been running for more than twenty years.

Another example comes from Buckley's marketers. Their cough syrup is nasty, and they are proud of it. They aren't trying to hide it. Instead, they made the bad taste the focus of their advertising campaign by comparing it to trash-bag leakage and sweaty gym socks. The tagline is "It tastes awful. And it works." However, the implicit message is that it works because it tastes awful.

Obviously, this approach won't work with everyone. Kironmoy Datta, senior brand manager for Novartis's consumer health products, says that "Buckley's isn't for everyone … We made a conscious choice to not be everything to everyone."

It takes courage to call attention to existing weaknesses, but it takes even more courage to exaggerate those weaknesses. That is what Hardee's did, and it saved their company. I found this letter from Andrew Puzder, president of Hardee's, on the back of the bag for my Philly Cheesesteak Thickburger.

A few years ago when I became president of Hardee's Restaurants, we were selling so many things that we had truly become a "jack of all trades and master of none." Unfortunately, in today's competitive fast food world, that wasn't cutting it.

The chain needed to become known for doing something really well again … So I challenged my menu development folks to come up with a new line of burgers that would make people say "Wow! I can't believe I can get burgers

> that good at a fast-food place." And they did. They came
> up with "Thickburgers."

It is important to note that Hardee's was going out of business and closing many of its stores before developing this new line of burgers. Even more important, most other fast-food companies were furiously adding healthy options to their menus. In response to criticism about the negative health effects of their offerings, fast-food outlets were offering water, fruit, and salads. Hardee's moved in the opposite direction.

In essence, Hardee's marketers were saying, "Our food is fat and nasty and will make you fat and nasty." And it worked. They succeeded by amplifying the weaknesses of fast food while everyone else was busy trying to moderate those same weaknesses. They took fast food—which was already tremendously unhealthy—and made it unhealthier. They took fatty foods and made them fattier. They took nasty food and made it nastier. And it worked.

Alignment and Avoidance

Amplification is only effective if you discover customers who want more of what you do well and don't care about what you don't do well. For example, the slogan for Alt Hotels in Canada is "We do less." The company's ads focus on what it doesn't do and what it does instead. For example, "We don't have a minibar. We do have a hip lounge." Alt Hotels is attracting the customers who want what it offers—a hip lounge—and repelling the customers who want what it doesn't offer—a minibar.

This is crucial. According to Frei and Morris, "Excellence requires underperforming on the things your customers value least, so you can over-deliver on the dimensions they value most." For example, most furniture stores have friendly and knowledgeable salespeople. They offer high-quality furniture that will last a lifetime. They will deliver it to your house and assemble it for you.

Compared to traditional furniture stores, IKEA underperforms. It has a lot of weaknesses. IKEA doesn't have salespeople. Its products are of lower quality and do not last a lifetime. IKEA doesn't deliver your furniture, and you have to assemble it yourself. So how is IKEA so successful?

IKEA succeeds by doing the opposite of most furniture stores. Furthermore, its employees have reframed their competition's strengths as weaknesses and reframed their own weaknesses as strengths. Salespeople can be helpful, but they can also make customers feel uncomfortable and pressured. IKEA doesn't pressure you. Purchasing lifetime furniture is expensive and a big commitment. IKEA's furniture is inexpensive and isn't a big commitment. You can also change it out when it goes out of style or breaks. Furniture delivery takes days and sometimes weeks; furniture from IKEA goes home with you today. Traditional furniture is assembled for you. Even though the process of assembling your IKEA furniture is frustrating, you have a sense of accomplishment from being involved.

Google and Yahoo are another great example of this process. Yahoo was the search engine leader before Google became the dominant force that it is today. So how did Google win? There are a lot of answers to that question, but one is particularly useful for our purposes. Look at Yahoo!'s home page. The first thing you probably notice is how full it is. There are innumerable links, stories, and banners. There's news, weather, sports, and more. Everything you need is right there.

Now, look at Google's home page. The first thing you probably notice is how empty it is. There is just a search box. Nothing you need is right there, so you'll have to search for it.

Google didn't try to beat Yahoo! by finding a way to put even more information, links, and advertisements on its home page. Instead, Google framed Yahoo!'s strengths as a weaknesses. Yahoo! wasn't informative; it was cluttered. Yahoo! wasn't helpful; it was confusing. Yahoo! told you what to read instead of helping you find what you wanted.

Google built a strength to compete with each of Yahoo!'s weaknesses. Google wasn't cluttered; it was clean and neat. Google wasn't confusing; it was simple. Google wasn't telling you where to go; it was there to help you find what you wanted.

Google dramatically underperformed compared to Yahoo!'s ability to put everything in one place, but this allowed them to better deliver on what many customers wanted: faster and more relevant searches.

Amplification and alignment ultimately come down to answering these questions:

→ **What does your company do well? How can you do even more?**

→ **Which customers love you? How can you create even deeper connections with them?**

➜ How can you invest more time, energy, and
   resources in your areas of strength?

Avoidance ultimately comes down to answering these questions:

➜ What does your company do poorly?
   How can you do it even worse?

➜ Which customers hate you? How can
   you make them even unhappier?

➜ How can you invest less time, energy, and
   resources in your areas of weakness?

Affiliation

There are all sorts of activities that can distract organizations from focusing on their unique competitive strengths. However, in many cases, it isn't possible to simply stop doing these activities. For example, offices need to be cleaned, taxes need to be paid, employees need to be hired, and products need to be shipped. In these cases, strategic partnerships, crowdsourcing, outsourcing, and/or mergers and acquisitions are options.

I don't think that it's necessary to discuss this further, because I'm not an expert in any of these areas (avoidance), and there are other good books on each of these topics. Additionally, most companies are already practicing affiliation at some level. For example, in chapter 7, I explained how I run my business by myself by hiring designers, web developers, publishers, and lawn services to do the things that I don't want to do.

The most important thing to remember is that even if a task is unavoidable, it doesn't have to be done by you or your company. It is often beneficial to hire or partner with another company that has competencies you lack instead of doing those things yourself. Individuals and organizations have limited time, energy, and resources. We need to use each wisely.

PART FOUR: LIVE

DIFFERENTLY

12. RELATIONSHIPS

Adventurous Al loves to take risks. He loves to explore and try new things. He loves to travel and rarely spends much time in one place. His work experience includes a variety of short-term jobs that he works just long enough to finance his next trip. This means that he has few assets or material possessions. For example, he doesn't own a car or a house. He doesn't even rent an apartment. If he needs a place to sleep, he just stays at a friend's house or in a cheap motel. He's quick to try any sport that is new and dangerous. He lives for the moment and has no plans for the future. During one of his trips, he meets a beautiful woman named Librarian Lucy.

Lucy loves stability and security. She carries a planner with a detailed list of things to do. Her goals are aligned with her long-term objectives. Lucy's career is steadily moving forward. Even though she is still in her twenties, she has money in her retirement plan and has already purchased a home. Her wedding is already planned, despite the fact that she is not even dating. She has even picked out the names of all her potential children. Lucy loves the routine and consistency of her life.

When Lucy and Al first met, they were instantly attracted to each other. We've all heard that opposites attract, but why does that happen? It seems that we are drawn to those characteristics that we don't have. We admire those qualities in the other person and wish we could be more like them. Al found Lucy attractive because she was everything he was not. Lucy found Al attractive because he was everything that she was not.

Additionally, Lucy is everything that people have told Al that he should be. People are always telling him that he needs to settle down and grow up. Similarly, Al is everything that people have told Lucy that she should be. People are always telling her that she needs to loosen up and take it easy. Their whole lives, they've been told that they should have the characteristics that the other person possesses. This is their chance to become better people.

So Al and Lucy got married and looked forward to a wonderful life together. Five years after their wedding, how are Al and Lucy doing? Do they still admire each other's unique qualities? Are they still in love?

Unfortunately, the answer is no. Al and Lucy can't stand to be together, and they are on the brink of divorce. How did this happen? The first answer is related to awareness.

Awareness

Has Lucy changed? No.

Is Al a different person? Again, the answer is no.

Lucy and Al's love didn't die because they didn't get what they bargained for. Al is still adventurous, and Lucy is still conservative. The difference is that they no longer see the other person in a positive light. They've lost their awareness of the other person's good qualities.

Furthermore, Lucy and Al have taken the very characteristics that created the initial attraction and turned them into negative qualities. Instead of seeing the good, they only see the bad.

Lucy used to see Al as easygoing, adventurous, and spontaneous. Now she sees him as irresponsible, dangerous, and impulsive.

→ **Easygoing** *became* **Irresponsible**

→ **Adventurous** *became* **Dangerous**

→ **Spontaneous** *became* **Impulsive**

Al used to see Lucy as structured, responsible, and cautious. Now he sees her as rigid, controlling, and fearful.

→ **Structured** *became* **Rigid**

→ **Responsible** *became* **Controlling**

→ **Cautious** *became* **Fearful**

These negative descriptions are simply the opposite of the very strengths that brought them together. Al and Lucy had hoped the other person's positive qualities would rub off on them; instead, they ended up rubbing them the wrong way.

This is negativity bias at work. We tend to see the down side, the dark side, of other people's good qualities. The difficulty is that both descriptions are true: Al is irresponsible and easygoing. Lucy is inflexible and structured. These characteristics are two sides of the same coin, and understanding this transforms our awareness. Since both descriptions are accurate, we can decide how we evaluate ourselves and others. This is the process of reframing that we discussed earlier.

I believe that we look at each other in relationships the same way that Al and Lucy looked at each other. We frame our partners' unique qualities in a negative way, and we miss the positive. We don't need to fix or remediate their qualities; that doesn't work anyway. It's a waste of our energy, and it leads to unhappiness. We need to accept both the strengths and corresponding weaknesses of our partners.

Acceptance

My grandparents are ninety-five years old and have been married for seventy years. They got married right after World War II and were farmers in central Wisconsin until they retired. It's easy to think that both members of a couple that has been married that long would have come to love and accept everything about the other person. But that isn't the case.

I had a chance to visit my grandparents recently, and my grandmother complained that my grandfather wasn't talking to her enough. He hasn't been talkative for the last seventy years, and yet my grandmother is still hopeful that he's about to change. This has been a source of conflict for nearly three quarters of a century, and she still hasn't been able to accept that she married an introverted man who doesn't have a lot to say. I think he secretly wishes that she'd stop talking, but he's too quiet to complain.

If seventy years isn't long enough to change something, then it probably isn't possible to do so. If a person hasn't changed after ninety-five years, they probably aren't going to change. I think that we can change ourselves and others, but we can't turn people into someone else. We can only help them to become more of who they are.

How could acceptance restore Al and Lucy's relationship? Lucy would stop trying to get Al to be more organized, responsible, and cautious. Al would stop trying to get Lucy to be more

312

easygoing, adventurous, and spontaneous. They would each acknowledge that the other person wasn't going to change and doesn't need to change. They would remind themselves of the strengths that correspond with each of their partner's weaknesses.

This might seem like a small and insignificant step, but it is very important. Our beliefs are powerful. Psychologists have demonstrated that actions are primarily based on thoughts and beliefs. People do what they think will work. Whether something works is usually measured by whether an action leads to positive feelings. In other words, people do what they think will make them feel good.

The "head, heart, and hands" model might clarify this process. Head represents your thoughts, heart represents your emotions, and hands represent your actions.

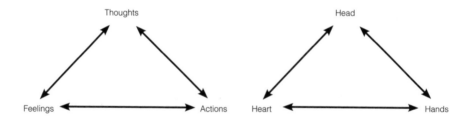

Negative thoughts about your partner (head) lead to negative feelings (heart) and then to negative actions (hands). Any effort to change your feelings or actions needs to begin with your beliefs. For example, if you focus on your partner's positive qualities (head), this will lead to more positive feelings (heart) and make it easier and more natural to treat him or her in positive ways (hands). Efforts to feel differently toward our partners or to treat them differently will be ineffective if we do not first change our thoughts.

I think that good relationships are built on acceptance of the other person's unique characteristics, both positive and negative. Great relationships go one step further: both people truly appreciate both sides of their partner's personality.

My primary point with acceptance is that you can't change your partner. The main point in appreciation is that you wouldn't want to change your partner if you clearly saw the connection between his or her best and worst traits.

Appreciation

Randy Pausch, a Carnegie Mellon professor, husband, and father of three young children, died of pancreatic cancer in 2008. His "Last Lecture" video has been viewed more than seventeen million times on YouTube, and his book, *The Last Lecture*, was a best seller. I was inspired and deeply moved by his story.

In the book, Pausch describes himself as arrogant, tactless, blunt, a know-it-all, an efficiency freak, and "a tough teacher with high expectations and some quirky ways ... I'm a bit of an acquired taste ... I had strengths that were also flaws." His good friend Scott Sherman described Pausch as a person who completely lacked tact and was likely to offend nearly anyone that he met. These unique characteristics, which some might see as weaknesses, are the primary reasons that he was recently included in The 100 Most Influential People in the World list by *Time* magazine.

After his wife, Jai, accidentally crashed one of their cars into their other car, Pausch didn't get upset. This surprised Jai, who was afraid that he would be angry with her. She was even more surprised and upset when he explained that he wasn't even going to get the cars fixed, since it was just body damage. Then he explained, "'You can't have just some of me, Jai,' I told her. 'You appreciate the part of me that didn't get angry because two things we own got hurt. But the flip side of that is my belief that you don't repair things if they still do what they are supposed to do.'" I love that line: "You can't have just some of me." Appreciation is seeing the weaknesses that frustrate us about the other person are connected to the strengths we admire.

What would appreciation look like for Al and Lucy? Lucy would begin to remember how much she admires Al's laid-back approach to life, his adventurous spirit, and his spontaneous nature. Al would remind himself how much he admires Lucy's responsibility, caution, and organization. They would each look for the ways in which their partner's differences make their lives together even richer. They would also communicate this appreciation verbally and in writing on a daily basis. Expressing appreciation will not only help their relationship, it will help their partner have more energy and confidence. Genuine appreciation is about loving the whole person and then helping him or her to become even more of who he or she is.

Amplification

If we truly appreciated our partners' unique qualities, then we would allow and even encourage them to turn up the volume on those qualities. Amplification starts with awareness. What are your partner's strength/weakness combinations from the assessment? How can you encourage him or her to maximize those strengths and at the same time make allowance for the corresponding weakness?

→ **If you encourage your partner's creativity, he or she will also be even more messy and disorganized.**

→ **If you encourage your partner's persistence, he or she will seem even more stubborn.**

→ **If you encourage your partner to be more thoughtful and reflective, he or she will get slower and more indecisive.**

But if we've learned acceptance and appreciation, these things won't be a problem. We can focus on the upside instead of the downside. We can handle the side effects because we understand the benefits.

This means that we need to stop trying to minimize or moderate our partners' weaknesses (acceptance). We don't need to try to make them more balanced and well-rounded. We don't need to change them just a little bit.

For example, Lucy could encourage Al to become even more easygoing, adventurous, and spontaneous. In turn, Al would encourage Lucy to become even more organized, responsible, and cautious. A natural result of this is that Al will begin to do things that are even more irresponsible, dangerous, and impulsive. Meanwhile, Lucy will begin to seem even more inflexible, controlling, and fearful.

This approach might seem like a recipe for disaster, but stay with me. I'll show you in the next couple sections how this seemingly ridiculous suggestion turns out. For example, one way to help our partners amplify their unique qualities is to help them find the right fit between who they are and what they do.

Alignment

My wife is a complainer—at least, that's what I thought for many years of our marriage. She was always talking about how things weren't good enough: The curtains in our dining room needed to be replaced. We needed a bigger deck. Our lawn wasn't lush enough. The carpet was wearing out. We should install wood floors.

This was especially surprising because we both grew up relatively poor. Her family never owned a home, their cars were unreliable, and they rarely had health insurance. I was born in a trailer park in Milwaukee. My family had just three bedrooms and one bathroom for six people. My brother and I had a bedroom in the living room, complete with a picture window and the front door to the house.

Because of this, I'm very satisfied with my life. My wife and I have a large home with individual bedrooms and a bathroom for each child. I couldn't understand why my wife didn't feel the same, and I was tired of her negativity.

My perspective changed after my wife and I completed the StrengthsFinder profile to help a friend who was doing coaching for Gallup. Her biggest strength is as a *maximizer*, which means that no matter how good things are, she wants to make them even better. This is crucial. She wasn't complaining; she was looking at the potential for improvement. Things can always be better. Things can always be improved, and my wife will always notice that.

Once I saw the strength (maximize) connected to her weakness (perfectionism and complaining), it transformed our relationship. Instead of feeling attacked and seeing her comments as critical and negative, I started seeing them as an accurate description of how to make things better and as an expression of one of her best qualities.

For my wife, alignment is having the opportunity to make things perfect. She loves to make the perfect meal, to design the perfect living room, to help our children dress perfectly, and to make sure that she looks perfect before she leaves the house. Alignment is also about doing activities that energize her instead of the ones that drain her. It's about using her strengths instead of fixing her weaknesses. For example, I've often wished that my wife would work with me on my speaking business. The problem is that she doesn't want to do presentations. She hates being up front. She doesn't want to design training programs. It isn't interesting to her. She doesn't want to manage the finances or logistics of the business, and she isn't particularly talented in those areas anyway. She definitely doesn't want to help with sales. She wouldn't like it, and she wouldn't do it well.

Many people would just take the perspective that it is my wife's responsibility to help make the family business a success, regardless of what she likes. But that violates the principle of alignment. If I'm going to teach the freak factor, then I have to live it as well. I know that making my wife miserable in order to make the business successful isn't going to lead to a better life.

I think that my wife should be an interior designer. Instead of helping me with my business, I'd love to see her start her own business. She comes alive when she talks about paint colors, counter surfaces, flooring, carpets, fabrics, furniture, and design. It energizes her and connects with her unique strengths. Alignment means that I don't pressure her to be something that she's not. Instead, I encourage her to find the right fit between who she is and what she does.

Alignment is also a crucial step in Al and Lucy's relationship. How can they amplify their strengths and weaknesses without killing each other? They need to find work that allows each of them to do what they do best, and they need to do it together.

Al and Lucy should start an adventure travel business. Al would lead the trips and help people have the greatest, most exciting adventures of their lives. He would be able to travel, take risks, and have more independence. Lucy would manage the business. She wouldn't have to take the trips. She would handle logistics. She would have the comfort and security of working near her home base and creating stability for the business. She could be responsible, organized, and cautious in the way she handled the organization's operations, while Al could be easygoing, adventurous, and spontaneous as he guided clients up frozen mountains and down white water rivers.

As we've already discussed, alignment applies to our career choices and to those of our partners. It also applies to parenting and hobbies. I've created a special section for parenting, so I won't spend a lot of time on that here. However, a simple example is that our differences as people can be expressed in our roles as parents. One partner might be more nurturing, and he or she can focus on those tasks. One partner might be more of a motivator, and he or she can focus on those tasks.

I think that we also need to allow our partners to have time and resources to focus on their own nonwork activities, such as hobbies and recreation. It's okay for my wife to have interests that I don't share and don't enjoy. I don't think it's necessary to do everything together. When she can do things that recharge her energy, we both win.

When my wife and I go on vacation, she has one goal: she wants to relax. On the other hand, I want to do as much as possible in the time we have. At the beginning of our marriage, she would complain that I wanted to do too much, and I would complain that she didn't want to do enough. Now we plan our vacations to include a few relaxing activities together as well as time for each of us to do what we enjoy the most. Stephanie will get a massage while I go on a hike in the mountains. Stephanie will sit by the pool while I play eighteen holes of golf. Stephanie will take a nap while I take surfing lessons. Each of us allows the other to recharge in a way that works for them instead of expecting them to do it our way.

Avoidance

Before we had our third daughter, my wife decided that she wanted to get a graduate degree in management. This meant that we'd need to take out $30,000 in student loans. I didn't hesitate, because it seemed like a good investment. But it would take more than money for her to graduate—it would take time, and I didn't have any. I was teaching full-time at one school and part-time at two graduate schools, all while building my business. In my spare time, I took care of our daughters so that Stephanie could study and write papers.

One night I was working on my laptop in the living room at 11 p.m. and noticed my wife moving the chairs out of the kitchen so that she could sweep and mop the floor. My first instinct was to tell her not to worry about it, but I knew that wouldn't work. She likes things to be clean (acceptance). I wanted to help, but I hate to clean and didn't have the time.

We had a choice to make. Was I going to sacrifice high-leverage activities (like building my business) and high-value activities (like spending time with my children) to become a maid? Or was Stephanie going to stop going to school in order to keep the house clean? Neither of these choices was acceptable (alignment).

So I did a quick calculation. With her master's degree, my wife could teach college courses on a part-time basis and earn at least $1,500 per class. It would cost $120 per month to hire someone to clean the house every two weeks. This meant that Stephanie could pay for almost a year of cleaning by teaching just one course. We hired a cleaning lady and never looked back (affiliation).

My wife and I didn't harass each other about failing to help. We didn't push each other to do even more. We didn't sacrifice what was really important. We did stop doing something that mattered less for something that mattered more.

What should Al and Lucy avoid? Al doesn't need to be involved in the finances and operations of the business. Lucy doesn't need to tell Al how to climb a mountain or skydive from a plane. Their relationship will be better and their lives will be more fulfilling when they each allow the other person to avoid activities which don't match their strengths.

JACK SPRAT COULD EAT NO FAT,

HIS WIFE COULD EAT NO LEAN.

AND SO BETWEEN THEM BOTH YOU SEE,

THEY LICKED THE PLATTER CLEAN.

Affiliation

This silly nursery rhyme is a good example of how partnerships at home can work effectively. My wife, Stephanie, is a great cook. She seems to have a natural gift for making food that tastes good even if she doesn't have the exact ingredients that the recipe requires. She also enjoys the creative process of putting together a complete meal (alignment). I don't like to do any of that. If it were up to me, I'd just eat food that didn't require any preparation. But we're a good team, because Stephanie hates to clean up after a meal. She's so exhausted from making it that she can't stand the thought of taking care of the mess. That is where I come in. I'm a finisher. I like to wrap things up. I like to get things done, especially small and manageable tasks (alignment).

However, it's easy to fail to appreciate this kind of partnership. I could complain that Stephanie never helps with the clean-up. She could complain that I never help with the cooking. Instead of accepting our unique roles and preferences, we could both spend our time complaining about what the other person doesn't do. But we don't. We try to find ways to let each person do what they do best and avoid those tasks that aren't a good fit. Everything needs to get done, but neither of us needs to do everything.

I've already explained how Al and Lucy could use affiliation to improve their relationship in the section on alignment, but I know some people might think that's unrealistic. So I'd like to share a real-life example.

Jason and Kim Kotecki are one of the best illustrations of affiliation that I've ever seen. They also demonstrate how the rest of the freak factor framework can improve relationships.

Jason is an artist, a professional speaker, and the author of *Penguins Can't Fly*. He and his wife, Kim (a former kindergarten teacher), have made it their mission in life to fight "adultitis" and help people use strategies from childhood to design lives with less stress and more fun.

Both Jason and Kim claim to be stubborn. "Our shared stubbornness has been vital to our persistence (appreciation). We worked on our business for five years before it could support us, and even then it was shaky for a few years after that." While making sacrifices and forgoing the normal comforts of existence, "there were times when we questioned our sanity." Stubbornness and persistence prevailed and allowed them to build their chosen lifestyle.

We both tend to be pretty silly and playful, which I imagine strikes some people as immature. But I see us as permission granters. Most people are yearning for a little silliness in their lives, but have abandoned their childlike ways by the time they get out in the "real world." When people see our example, it gives them permission to let their hair down and add a little bit more fun and adventure into their own lives.

Jason and Kim have learned that the creation of books, blog posts, and business models requires a deployment of their freakish qualities of stubbornness and silliness. This is both challenging and freeing.

When I (Jason) was younger I was criticized for being too much of a daydreamer. But I have come to see what a strength that really is. The ideas and innovations I've come up with are the primary engine that has driven our business to where it is today. Of course, not every idea works—most don't—but visioning [sic] and innovation take time. Sometimes the time spent yields very little result and you can feel like you're wasting your time. Kim has been a big champion of me taking time to "daydream," because she knows the good that can come from it.

I (Jason) am much better at dealing with big picture things than the details and I hate doing repetitive tasks. And the phone—I hate the phone! Fortunately, Kim is well-suited for details and repetition and systems. And she shines on the phone. Her warm, inviting, and bubbly personality serves her—and our company—well as she sells our speaking programs and manages customer relationships. I've often joked that she's the perfect salesperson, because who can say no to a kindergarten teacher?

[Kim remembers her training ground.] Before my full-time commitment to our company, I spent 5 years as a kindergarten teacher. Being detail-oriented and organized, I've shifted from preparing down to the minute details of my day with 25 five and six years olds, to preparing down to the minute details of Jason's travel and speaking schedule. People could argue that at times the level of detail I put into these projects can be a bit obsessive (amplification) with hints of perfectionism and I would assure you that it better! Publicity, travel, invoicing, proposals and marketing – it all requires an attention to detail that I am able to provide and enjoy doing it (alignment).

My attention span can be a bit scattered and short at times. When I was teaching, I was very accustomed to changing activities every five minutes, to keep the interest of the kiddos. Some would say that this is not effective in a business because I'm easily distracted and lack focus. This trait actually works in my favor within my role in our company because I am constantly being interrupted by client requests and potential client inquiries. I try to respond to our client requests promptly, so it's not uncommon for me to interrupt a project I'm working on in order to meet their needs and return to my original task. Our clients love the personal attention, and I am still able to complete everything by the end of the day.

Jason and Kim have built a business that allows both of them to amplify their unique qualities and create alignment between who they are and what they do. This business partnership has a positive impact on their relationship as well.

13. PARENTING

A number of years ago, my friend's wife, Lynn, asked me to do a parenting presentation for a women's group. I was happy to do the talk, but I was a little apprehensive. Because the meeting was just for women, I would be the only man in the room.

To make matters worse, at the time of the presentation, I didn't have any children. My only qualifications were academic, since I had undergraduate and graduate degrees in counseling psychology. This probably wouldn't count for much since I already had two major strikes against me. I was a man with no children who would be telling mothers and grandmothers how to care for their offspring.

Fortunately, Lynn assured me that my failure to procreate would not be a problem. She had an introduction that would give me the credibility I needed to win over the audience. She started by listing my qualifications and then explained that I had been a friend of her husband's since high school. Apparently, he had shared many stories with her about my past, and his revelations had led her to an important conclusion.

The final words of her introduction were, "The reason you should listen to Dave is because he is proof that even your really bad kids can turn out okay." Ouch! In other words, she was saying that I had secret knowledge about the inner workings of difficult children. Maybe I had some special insights to share from my checkered past.

I want to focus on Lynn's final phrase—I'm a bad kid who turned out okay. How exactly did that happen? Was I really a bad kid? What lessons can we learn from that experience that will improve our parenting? As you know from reading the rest of the book, I turned out okay by applying the freak factor framework. Let's start with awareness.

Awareness

When it comes to parenting, there are two levels of awareness. The first is your ability to identify your children's strengths and weaknesses. The second is your children's understanding of their own strengths and weaknesses.

You can use the assessment in chapter 2 to improve your awareness of your children's unique characteristics and the connections between their weaknesses and strengths. However, I have also created an assessment for children to do on their own or with your help. Additionally, I made a list of questions to help children improve their self-awareness and think about how they can apply their distinctive qualities.

1. What is something you are good at?

Something I am good at is _____.

2. What is something you do that other people don't like?

Something I do that others don't like is _____.

3. What is something that you wish you could change about yourself?

I wish I could change _____ about myself.

4. How can you do the opposite of what everyone else is doing?

I can do the opposite of what everyone else is doing by _____
_____.

5. How can you get even better at something you do well?

I can make something I am good at even better by _____
_____.

6. How can you stick out instead of trying to fit in?

I can stick out instead of trying to fit in by _____
_____.

7. Of everything you have done, what is the one thing you are the most proud of?

Of everything I have done, I am the most proud of _____
_____.

8. What was the happiest day of your life? What were you doing?

The happiest day of my life was when _____
_____.

9. What is your favorite subject in school? Which part do you like best?

My favorite subject in school is _____ because _____
_____.

10. What is your favorite job or chore? What do you like best about it?

My favorite job or chore is _____ because _____
_____.

11. What job or chore do you hate to do? What do you hate about it?

The job or chore I hate to do is _____ because _____
_____.

12. What subject in school do you dislike? Which part do you hate the most about it?

The subject in school I dislike is _____ because
_____.

13. Which kind of activities do you put off doing until you have to?

An activity I put off doing until I have to is _____
_____.

14. What activities make you tired?

I get tired when I have to _____.

1. Put check marks in the boxes next to your strengths (a strength is something that is good about you).

2. If you notice a trait that is definitely not one of your strengths, draw a line through it.

3. Choose your top three strengths.

x	Strengths	x	Strengths
	1. I am **creative** and have new ideas about how something can be done.		14. I am **independent** and do things without help from others.
	2. I am **organized**. When I do something, I am careful and pay attention to details.		15. I am a **team player** and am more concerned for other people than I am for myself.
	3. I am **dedicated**. I try to do something even though it is difficult or other people want me to stop.		16. I am **sensitive**. I am caring.
	4. I am **flexible**. I can adapt in order to fit in or work better in a situation.		17. I am **humble**. I do not think of myself as better than other people.
	5. I am **enthusiastic**. I express strong emotions.		18. I am **confident** and do not worry a lot.
	6. I am **calm**. I am relaxed.		19. I am **spontaneous**. I make decisions quickly.
	7. I have a lot of **energy**. I am very active.		20. I am a **leader**. I can influence other people.
	8. I am **thoughtful** and think carefully about things.		21. I am **relaxed**. I am easygoing.
	9. I am **adventurous**. I am very brave.		22. I am **serious**. I am mature.
	10. I am **responsible**. I am careful about avoiding danger and risk.		23. I am **funny**. I am amusing.
	11. I am **honest**. I do not waste time, and I get right to the point.		24. I am **generous**. I like to use what I have to help others.
	12. I am **polite**. I am respectful. I am courteous.		25. I am **curious**. I have a desire to know and learn more.
	13. I am **competitive** and determined to win.		

#1 Strength: _____

#2 Strength: _____

#3 Strength: _____

Directions

1. Put check marks in the boxes next to your weaknesses (a weakness is something that is not good about you).

2. If you notice a trait that is definitely not one of your weaknesses, draw a line through it.

3. Choose your top three weaknesses.

x	Weaknesses	x	Weaknesses
	1. I am sloppy and **messy**. I am disorganized.		14. I am **selfish**. I only care about myself.
	2. I don't like to change.		15. I need a lot of help from others. I need a lot of attention.
	3. I am **stubborn**.		16. I am **easily hurt**. I am easily upset.
	4. I have a hard time keeping my promises.		17. I am **not confident** about myself or my abilities.
	5. I become **angry** quickly and easily.		18. I have too much pride in myself. I am **overconfident**.
	6. I am not **sympathetic** toward other people.		19. I am **impatient**. I don't like to wait. I do things without thinking.
	7. I **worry** a lot. I usually feel nervous.		20. I am **bossy**. I'm always telling people what to do.
	8. I am quiet. I am **shy**.		21. I am **lazy**.
	9. I **don't worry** about the consequences of my actions.		22. I am **too serious**. I am not very fun.
	10. I am boring. I am not very interesting.		23. I am **too silly**. I am immature.
	11. I am rude. I am not polite.		24. I am **easily fooled**. I am easily tricked.
	12. I don't always tell people how I really feel. I don't want to hurt their feelings.		25. I am **nosy**. I get too involved in other people's business.
	13. I care about winning more than anything else.		

#1 Weakness: _____

#2 Weakness: _____

#3 Weakness: _____

Acceptance

Parents have a powerful influence on their children. However, this influence can sometimes be quite negative. In his book *The Element*, Ken Robinson tells the story of Paulo Coelho, a young man who wanted to be a writer. Unfortunately, Paulo's parents thought that he should be a lawyer and that writing was nothing more than a hobby. When Paulo resisted their advice and pursued his writing career, his parents had him committed to a psychiatric institution, where he was given electroshock treatments.

Paulo's parents did this because they loved him and wanted what was best for him. But their notions of what was best included having a normal life with a good job that paid a good salary for doing respectable work. They believed that their job as parents was to change Paulo from who he was (and who he wanted to be) into who they felt he should be. They weren't able to accept his uniqueness.

Matt Langdon of The Hero Construction Company teaches kids that they can be heroes in everyday situations. One of Langdon's posts about the movie *The Tale of Despereaux* argues that it is good to be strange. The post begins with a quote from the movie, which is a cartoon about a mouse with extraordinarily large ears and tremendous courage.

"Reader, you must know that an interesting fate awaits almost everyone, mouse or man, who does not conform." When you act heroically, you're going to stand out. Despereaux's ears were not the only thing that made people notice him. His courage, thoughts of a better world, and kindness made him stand out. They also made him the object of disdain and mockery. Heroes are ordinary people who do extraordinary things, so there will always be a majority to [sic] think the hero's behavior is wrong, dangerous, or weird. Heroes don't cower and they don't subscribe to the ideas of the masses just because those ideas are popular.

If we want our children to be extraordinary, we need to make sure that we aren't implicitly or explicitly forcing them to conform to narrow standards of normalcy.

Remember negativity bias? When your child brings home a report card, what do you focus on? Do you talk about the good grades or the bad grades? Do you try to build on their strengths or fix their weaknesses?

I once brought home a report card with an A in every subject except English; I was getting a C in that class. How did my parents respond? Did they compliment me on my excellent work in most of my classes? Did they encourage me to focus my efforts on those areas where I was having success? No. Instead, they wanted to talk about English. What was I doing wrong? How could I do better? Was I trying hard enough? They believed, as most parents do, that we all need to be well-rounded.

The people who are closest to us are the ones most likely to uncover and address our deepest flaws. We might be able to hide some weaknesses from others, but our families tend to know us better than anyone else.

Acceptance begins by recognizing that our children's weaknesses are also strengths. It is about seeing the upside instead of just the downside. Let's continue the assessment and try to find the connections between your child's weaknesses and strengths.

1. Make a list of the top three strengths and weaknesses that you identified in the awareness section.

2. Put a check mark next to each of them on the chart below.

3. Are there any matches? A match is when you selected a strength and a weakness in the same row.

X	Strengths	Weaknesses	X
	1. I am creative and have new ideas about how something can be done.	1. I am sloppy and messy. I am disorganized.	
	2. I am organized. When I do something, I am careful and pay attention to details.	2. I don't like to change.	
	3. I am dedicated. I try to do something even though it is difficult or other people want me to stop.	3. I am stubborn.	
	4. I am flexible. I can adapt in order to fit or work better in a situation.	4. I have a hard time keeping my promises.	
	5. I am enthusiastic. I express strong emotions.	5. I become angry quickly and easily.	
	6. I am calm. I am relaxed.	6. I am not sympathetic toward other people.	
	7. I have a lot of energy. I am very active.	7. I worry a lot. I usually feel nervous.	
	8. I am thoughtful and think carefully about things.	8. I am quiet. I am shy.	

x	Strengths	Weaknesses	x
	9. I am adventurous. I am very brave.	9. I don't worry about the consequences of my actions.	
	10. I am responsible. I am careful about avoiding danger and risk.	10. I am boring. I am not very interesting.	
	11. I am honest. I do not waste time, and I get right to the point.	11. I am rude. I am not polite.	
	12. I am polite. I am respectful. I am courteous.	12. I don't always tell people how I really feel. I don't want to hurt their feelings.	
	13. I am competitive and determined to win.	13. I care about winning more than anything else.	
	14. I am independent and do things without help from others.	14. I am selfish. I only care about myself.	
	15. I am a team player. I'm more concerned for other people than I am for myself.	15. I need a lot of help from others. I need a lot of attention.	
	16. I am sensitive. I am caring.	16. I am easily hurt. I am easily upset.	
	17. I am humble. I do not think of myself as better than other people.	17. I am not confident about myself or my abilities.	
	18. I am confident and do not worry a lot.	18. I have too much pride in myself. I am overconfident.	
	19. I am spontaneous. I make decisions quickly.	19. I am impatient. I don't like to wait. I do things without thinking.	
	20. I am a leader. I can influence other people.	20. I am bossy. I'm always telling people what to do.	
	21. I am relaxed. I am easygoing.	21. I am lazy.	
	22. I am serious. I am mature.	22. I am too serious. I am not very fun.	
	23. I am funny. I am amusing.	23. I am too silly. I am immature.	
	24. I am generous. I like to use what I have to help others.	24. I am easily fooled. I am easily tricked.	
	25. I am curious. I have a desire to know and learn more.	25. I am nosy. I get too involved in other people's business.	

Appreciation

Appreciation isn't always easy. My youngest daughter, Sophia, was at her first day of kindergarten. At snack time, the teacher asked each child if they had something to eat and drink. Sophia told the teacher that she had a snack; we had packed some crackers and a small bottle of water. But then something unexpected happened. A few of the kids didn't have snacks. They had either forgotten, or their parents weren't aware that they needed one.

The teacher didn't want these kids to be left out, so she gave some cookies and juice to each of the kids who didn't have a snack. Sophia didn't like that at all. She had been responsible and brought her snack, but it was just plain crackers and water. Now these kids, who hadn't followed the rules, were getting rewarded with juice and cookies. She wanted juice and cookies, but she'd already told the teacher she had a snack. What could she do?

Sophia raised her hand. When the teacher called on her, she said, "I forgot. I'm allergic to water." This is funny, but it is also disconcerting. This wasn't Sophia's first lie. She lies regularly, even about things that don't matter. It would be easy to start to see her as a bad person—as fundamentally dishonest. But there is another perspective.

Researchers have found a link between dishonesty and intellectual development in children. In other words, it takes a certain level of intelligence to tell a good lie and children can't lie until their brain has reached a particular stage of development. Additionally, people with higher IQs tend to lie more often.

There's something else you should know about Sophia: she is very imaginative. For example, she has innumerable dolls and stuffed animals, and she can play with them for hours, making up elaborate stories about their pretend adventures. This doesn't mean that I condone her dishonesty or tell her that it's acceptable to lie. I don't. However, I do see that there is an upside. I appreciate the strengths (imagination and intelligence) that correspond to this particular weakness (dishonesty). I haven't branded her as a bad child, because I see that there's another side to the story.

Sophia is also very stubborn. This can be very frustrating. When you tell her that she can't have something, she will continue asking you incessantly in the hope that she will wear you down. As much as I don't like to admit this, there is an upside to this as well. She is very persistent.

My job as a parent is to acknowledge, appreciate, and encourage Sophia's persistence, because I know that it is a positive trait which will serve her very well as an adult. Again, it is my prerogative to tell her that I don't appreciate being nagged and to avoid giving in to her, but I shouldn't criticize her as stubborn and tell that it is a bad trait that she needs to eliminate. That isn't true, and it's not helpful.

Amplification

If we truly appreciated our children's unique qualities, we would find ways to help them exaggerate those qualities. We would help them amplify instead of moderating or minimizing their unusual characteristics.

Adam's parents remember that he was always screaming as a child. Adam explains, "Apparently, I was a real pain in the butt in restaurants. They couldn't take me anywhere. I was super super noisy ... I was very talkative, very hyperactive. I was bouncing off the walls all the time. Not much different than I am now really." He was noisy, so they told him to be quiet. They even stopped taking him out, because it was embarrassing to have a child who wasn't normal and quiet and obedient.

Adam has grown up, but he's still screaming and noisy. Now he has a full band and sound system to accompany him and amplify his voice. I'd bet that his parents are happy that he didn't listen when they told him to be quiet, because Adam Lambert was the runner-up on American Idol in 2009. Lambert's first album sold nearly a million copies worldwide—more sales than Kris Allen, the 2009 winner.

We shouldn't wait until someone else helps our children amplify their strengths and weaknesses. It's possible that no one ever will. We need to be the ones who encourage our children to be more of who they are.

Alignment

Last year, I was watching the classic TV version of *Rudolph the Red-Nosed Reindeer* and realized that it beautifully illustrates the importance of alignment and of finding the right fit.

"Rudolph the red-nosed reindeer had a very shiny nose, and if you ever saw it, you would even say it glows."

Rudolph was different. He had a major and obvious flaw. He was a freak. This is the same for most of us. We are different. We have flaws. We are too impatient or too messy or too organized or too serious or too loud or too quiet. We are freaks.

"All of the other reindeer used to laugh and call him names. They never let poor Rudolph join in any reindeer games."

Rudolph's flaw made him unpopular and led to his rejection and isolation. No one wants to be rejected. So what do we do? We often try to hide our flaws and fix our weaknesses. We become ashamed. We wish that we could just be normal, like everyone else. We want to be accepted, so we try to change.

This is just what Rudolph and his parents tried to do. They covered up his nose with a black rubber cone, but it didn't work. His red nose still shone through. It looked like Rudolph was destined for a life of pain and misery, but the situation changed.

"Then one foggy Christmas Eve, Santa came to say, Rudolph with your nose so bright, won't you guide my sleigh tonight?"

Rudolph's nose wasn't really a weakness. It was a strength in disguise. In the right situation—a "foggy Christmas Eve"—Rudolph's nose was an irreplaceable advantage. When the situation changed, the value of his unique characteristic changed as well.

What made Rudolph a freak also made him a hero. He didn't succeed in spite of his weakness; he succeeded because of his weakness. What would have happened if Rudolph had gone to Hollywood and gotten a nose job?

"Then all the reindeer loved him, and they shouted out with glee, Rudolph the Red-Nosed Reindeer, you'll go down in history."

Rudolph's legacy, his enduring fame, was the result of a perfect fit between his unique qualities and the situation.

Do you want your children to succeed? Do you want them to make history or at least make a difference? Help them find their foggy Christmas Eve. Look to their apparent weaknesses and flaws—they are strengths in disguise. They offer clues to how your children can make a unique contribution. Don't try to hide them or fix them. Just find the right situation: the one that offers the perfect fit between who they are and what is required. Unlike Rudolph, we don't have to just wait for the right situation to come along; we can seek it out or even create it.

Michael Phelps is the most successful Olympian of all time. He has more medals than anyone else. But he also has ADHD, so when Phelps was growing up, his mom had a decision to make. Should she give him medicine to "fix" his ADHD, or should she help him find a situation that rewarded him for his hyperactivity? Athletics is a situation that rewards children for the same characteristics that they are punished for at school. Phelps's mom realized that she didn't need to change him; she needed to change the situation. If she couldn't change who he was, then she could change where he was.

When it comes to kids, one of the problems with alignment is that school is a single, very specific situation that lasts for their entire childhood. A failure to fit in at school can leave parents and children feeling like failures. But as we have seen many times in this book, how a person does in school isn't always a predictor of the level of success they will achieve in life. Furthermore, even though we spend most of our childhood in school, we spend most of our life outside of school.

Nevertheless, school success is a major concern for many parents. Here are a few suggestions:

Start by considering alternative schools, such as those focusing on art, music, drama, dance, or engineering. Montessori schools, online education, and home schooling are other options. Unconventional education can be a good fit for unconventional kids.

If alternative schooling isn't an option—and for many parents, it isn't—there are other things you can do. Look for extracurricular activities within the school that are a good match for your child's unique qualities. Sports, band, debate, choir, student government, and many other activities help kids who don't fit in to find a place where they do fit. If you can't change the larger situation (school), try to find or create other situations that give your child a different and more positive perspective on his or her strengths and weaknesses.

If your child gets in trouble at school for misbehavior, the way you respond to that at home has a big impact on your child. I got punished again at home for things I had already been punished for at school. The message was clear: if the teacher thinks you are bad, then you are bad.

We need to be careful when we give other adults this kind of power to decide what is good or bad about our child. Sometimes we need to contextualize the misbehavior. For example, a teacher might say that your child is immature and has no self-control, because he or she talks too much. You can support the teacher's right to manage the class in the way he or she sees fit, but you should also let your child know that his or her behavior, although inappropriate in that situation, is also evidence of positive qualities that can be used at the right place and the right time.

The next thing to do is to create the right place and the right time for your child to be unique. I was always being told that this wasn't the time or place for me to be myself. But it seemed like the time never came, and we never arrived at the place. If your children are hyper, get them more time in the yard and on the playground. Sign them up for local sports teams. If your children are creative but messy, get them in an art class. Help them to discover where they fit. Give them outlets for their uniqueness.

Avoidance

My oldest daughter, Anna, isn't very athletic. She isn't very coordinated. She doesn't like groups and the chaos of team sports. She is independent. She doesn't like to get sweaty. She doesn't want to get hurt. She isn't competitive. When it was time to sign up for fall or spring sports at her school, we would ask her if she wanted to play. She always declined. One year, when we asked her about it, she said, "Sports just isn't my thing."

Although I was very athletic and I know the value of sports, I never forced her to join a team. I allowed her to avoid activities that weren't a good fit. This is the other side of alignment. We need to help our kids find the right fit, and we also need to allow them to avoid activities that don't match their interests and abilities. It needs to be okay for them to say that something is "not their thing."

When she was in sixth grade, Anna signed up for the new swimming team. It was the perfect fit (alignment): she is tall and thin. Swimming is repetitive and doesn't require a lot of coordination. It is very safe. She isn't going to get hit with a ball or fall on the ground. She can be independent—swimming requires a very low level of teamwork and cooperation. It's also hard to get sweaty in the pool.

This brings us to the subject of quitting. Sometimes kids don't realize that something isn't their thing until they've already started. As we've already discussed, I'm a big fan of quitting. I think that it's great to encourage kids to try new things: How else will they know what they like and what they don't like? Experimentation is an important part of developing their self-awareness. However, they'll be less open to trying new things if we have an absolute "no quitting" policy. My youngest daughter has quit soccer, dance, and gymnastics. She still hasn't found her thing, but she will.

Affiliation

Home is a great place to learn teamwork. It's a great place for kids to learn that they don't have to do everything and that different people can work together to accomplish mutual goals. Look for opportunities to use your children's complementary strengths. For example, maybe one of your kids is very organized and does a great job loading the dishwasher to maximum capacity. Another kid loves to be outside and enjoys yard work. We don't need to force each child to do an equal amount of the same work; we can allow them each to contribute by using their unique strengths.

The main idea is that childhood is a great time to learn about both interdependence and uniqueness. We can help our kids learn to contribute to a group objective by offering their best individual talents.

Preserving the Tilt

In 1173, the people who began building the Leaning Tower of Pisa had some trouble creating a stable foundation. It started tipping over before they'd even finished building the second floor. The builders tried to fix it but couldn't get it to straighten up. That was a very lucky break for the city of Pisa.

Millions of people have spent millions of dollars to visit the city for one reason: to see a tower that leans. The problem those builders tried to fix is the very reason that so many people travel to this otherwise somewhat obscure location. As one of the many websites devoted to the tower explains, "Because of its inclination, and its beauty, from 1173 up to the present the Tower has been the object of very special attention."

Even so, some people just can't handle a broken tower. In 1934, Benito Mussolini declared that the tower should be straightened. Fortunately, the effort to fix the tower failed and actually caused it to lean even more. In 1964, the Italian government took steps to keep the tower from falling down. However, this time they decided that it was "important to keep the current tilt, due to the vital role that this element played in promoting the tourism industry of Pisa."

There are four important lessons we can learn from the Leaning Tower of Pisa. First, people go to see the tower because of its obvious flaw, not in spite of that flaw. Its weakness is its strength. The tower's flaw is "vital" and has made it the "object of very special attention."

Second, fixing the flaw would destroy the tower's uniqueness, but that hasn't kept people from trying. Third, efforts to fix flaws usually fail. Fourth, it is worth the effort to maintain the flaw, to preserve the inclination, and "to keep the current tilt."

Other people will always try to get you to straighten up. They will call you a freak. They will frame your strengths as weaknesses and demand that you fix them.

Don't pay attention to them. Just keep leaning.

This book started with a quote from e. e. cummings: "We do not believe in ourselves until someone reveals that deep inside us something is valuable, worth listening to, worthy of our trust, sacred to our touch."

It is my mission in life to reveal to people that deep inside them something is valuable, worth listening to, worthy of our trust, and sacred to our touch. I want to create a freak revolution in our homes, schools, and workplaces, but I need your help.

You can be part of the revolution by doing the following:

- → Apply what you've learned in this book.
- → Share the book with others.
- → Read *The Freak Factor for Kids* to your children.
- → Join the Freak Revolution at drendall.com.
- → Bring me in to speak at a school or company event.
- → Connect with me on LinkedIn.
- → Become my friend on Facebook.